THE BEATEN PATH

Other Books by PTOLEMY TOMPKINS
Paradise Fever
This Tree Grows Out of Hell

PTOLEMY TOMPKINS

THE BEATEN PATH

FIELD NOTES ON GETTING WISE
IN A WISDOM-CRAZY WORLD

wm

WILLIAM MORROW
75 YEARS OF PUBLISHING
An Imprint of HarperCollins*Publishers*

THE BEATEN PATH. Copyright © 2001 by Ptolemy Tompkins. All rights reserved.
Printed in the United States of America. No part of this book may be used or
reproduced in any manner whatsoever without written permission except in the
case of brief quotations embodied in critical articles and reviews. For information address HarperCollins Publishers Inc., 10 East 53rd Street,
New York, NY 10022.

HarperCollins books may be purchased for educational, business, or sales
promotional use. For information please write: Special Markets Department,
HarperCollins Publishers Inc., 10 East 53rd Street, New York, NY 10022.

FIRST EDITION

Designed by Fearn Cutler

Printed on acid-free paper

Library of Congress Cataloging-in-Publication Data
Tompkins, Ptolemy.
The beaten path : field notes on getting wise in a wisdom-crazy world /
Ptolemy Tompkins.—1st ed.
p.   cm.
Includes index.
ISBN 0-380-97822-9
1. Spiritual life.   I. Title
BL624 .T65   2001
299'.93—dc21
[B]   00-048976

01   02   03   04   05   RRD   10   9   8   7   6   5   4   3   2   1

PERMISSIONS

For my mother,

Rebecca, and

Francie

Life is a festival only to the wise.

—EMERSON

CONTENTS

ACKNOWLEDGMENTS

Many books were indispensable in the making of this book about books. The pages devoted to Taoism owe much to Toshihiko Izutsu's *Sufism and Taoism: A Comparative Study of Key Philosophical Ideas*. Further assistance in understanding the concept of Hun Tun came from N. J. Girardot's *Myth and Meaning in Early Taoism*. Richard de Mille's books on Castaneda—*Castaneda's Journey* and *The Don Juan Papers*—were central not only in helping me to grapple with the Carlos Castaneda enigma but also in providing many of the initial ideas and insights that got me started on the project. Monica Furlong's *Zen Effects: The Life of Alan Watts* gave me an invaluable full-color portrait of Watts the man to puzzle over. The pages on Aldous Huxley benefited much from David King Dunaway's *Huxley in Hollywood*. The writings of Huston Smith, Jacob Needleman, Frithjof Schuon, E. F. Schumacher, and Richard Tarnas, though generally not alluded to in the book, were tutelary forces at one point or another.

ACKNOWLEDGMENTS

So much for the books. As for people: Thanks first and foremost to Howard Yoon, Rachel Klayman, and Robin and Stuart Ray. Without them, no book. Thanks also to my editor at Morrow, Jennifer Brehl, my agent, Gail Ross, Josh Horwitz, David Reynolds, Matthew Hamilton, Jocasta Brownlee, Rosemary Davidson, Philip Zaleski, T. C. Tompkins, Oliver Ray, Joyce Wong, Jack Weiner, Jerree Tompkins, Greg Mirhej, Karl Greenfeld, Nicky Vreeland, Maria Teresa Train, Marvin Barrett, Maura Maguire, Susan Heckler, Ralph White, Cathy Mars, Leah Zanoni, and Paul and Zack, the book merchants of Washington Square Park, who supplied me with fresh copies of many a long-lost Life Manual. Last but not least, thanks to my wife, Rebecca, for putting up with a husband more neurotic than wise, and more troublesome than tranquil.

INTRODUCTION

Of making many books there is no end.

—ECCLESIASTES

I have a funny relationship with wisdom. This is, I believe, because I have been born into a funny moment in the history of the stuff—a time when there is both more and less of it available than ever before, and when getting wisdom for oneself is both an unprecedentedly promising and an unprecedentedly hopeless project.

Why is so much wisdom available today? Because it is now, to an extent that it has never been before, a product—something you can buy, sell, and carry around in your back pocket; something that can be taught at seminars, concentrated into videocassettes, and broadcast on-line in daily installments. If you want to know why things are the way they are, and if you like the idea of hearing this news from a single, dog-eared, trustworthy volume, such volumes are available in a quantity and variety that no other generation at any other time or place in history has ever known.

Among the great majority of cultures that came before ours,

the issue of where to go for answers to life's essential dilemmas never came up. No young member of a primitive society, perched on the edge of adulthood and wondering about the meaning of life and his or her place in it, ever had to choose between Iranian Sufism, Japanese Zen, Amerindian shamanism, and Tibetan Buddhism as a source of insight into these questions. The culture of such a person would typically have been structured around a single mythic system, and that system would have informed, to a greater or lesser degree, every aspect of his or her existence. If this individual was inclined to ask questions about life's ultimate meaning, all the answers would have been in the myths. The idea of shopping around for a better set of them would simply not have arisen.

Not that these myths always made immediate sense upon first hearing. In fact, mastery of their meanings and mysteries could take a lifetime. But regardless of how daunting, confusing, or strange the materials in the communal wisdom bank sounded to begin with, it was always understood that they *did* contain the answers. If you had the energy to persevere—to live and wrestle with the myths daily—you would eventually find what you hungered for.

When the oral myths and legends of preliterate peoples eventually began to take up residence within the covers of books, exactly the same trust and respect for the material continued to prevail. Western civilization's first books were wisdom books—specifically, the various works of Near Eastern wisdom, formerly stored on scrolls, that came to make up the Bible—and since their first appearance books and wisdom have been synonymous. The volumes that people have carried with them longest and cherished the most have always been the wise ones: those that contain the kind of core insights that help make the bumps and turns of life more navigable, its joys and miseries more understandable. And, just as was the case with myth in preliterate times, a given culture tended to have *one* book from which they expected all the answers to come.

In *A Guide for the Perplexed*, a great attempt at summarizing the collective wisdom of the premodern world and making its imperatives intelligible to modern readers, E. F. Schumacher wrote that "it may conceivably be possible to live without churches; but it is not possible to live without religion, that is, without systematic work to keep in contact with, and develop toward, Higher Levels than those of 'ordinary life' with all its pleasure or pain, sensation, gratification, refinement or crudity—whatever it may be. *The modern experiment to live without religion has failed,* and once we have understood this, we know what our 'post modern' tasks really are."

One of the first among those tasks, Schumacher made clear, is to recover a series of genuine maps-for-transformed-living: maps which allow people today, especially young people, to make themselves worthy of a world that is indeed larger, stranger, and more ripe with hidden promise than the perspective of mere "ordinary life" could ever comprehend. Schumacher wrote *A Guide for the Perplexed* in the late seventies, and since then the maps have been coming in hard and heavy. In fact, there are more of them floating around now than ever before. Unfortunately, for all their abundance, these maps don't seem to be able to speak to us in the same way that they did back in the times when there was essentially one wisdom source per culture, and when the centrality of that source was taken completely for granted. The wisdom book of times and cultures past—difficult, intractable, and demanding a lifetime's study to be genuinely understood—has given way to the popular wisdom book of today: an appealingly packaged, highly digestible, and more often than not entirely unthreatening commodity, easy to buy and destined to lose at least some of its punch by the time the next season's offerings are on sale. With the world's primordial and traditional wisdom systems in disarray and the hunger for wisdom being fed by this burst of market-driven material, the situation is much like that of an old-growth forest that has been leveled overnight. On the ground, newly exposed to the sunlight, a rich profusion of growth is springing up. But unlike the trees that it has replaced, this growth is fragile, its roots tentative, and its nutritional content sometimes questionable in the extreme. So it is that in spite of the seeming ease of acquiring wisdom these days—and for all the variety and appeal of the packages it comes in—there is something unprecedentedly difficult about actually getting this material *into* ourselves in a lasting and meaningful way.

Though we seem to be living in the Golden Age of wisdom books, America's love affair with them is not entirely new. The essential religiosity of Americans, combined with their love of novelty, has long made books of refurbished or rephrased wisdom popular here, and sales-conscious mystics have been around at least since Walt Whitman. But the first real burst of market-savvy wisdom books—the ones that plunged into the wisdom troves of ages past, reformulated them, and presented ready-to-use information to book buyers anxious for advice on life and how it should be lived—occurred in the early sixties, right around the time I was born.

From the original to the ancient, from the easy to the obscure, from the good to the lousy, the wisdom book as a mass phenomenon was born: the *Tao-te Ching;* the *I Ching; The Way of Zen; Be Here Now; The Perennial Philosophy;* The Tibetan Book of the Dead; *The Teachings of Don Juan; Black Elk Speaks;* the *Bhagavad Gita; Zen Mind, Beginner's Mind; Zen and the Art of Motorcycle Maintenance; Zen in the Art of Archery; Notes to Myself; Jonathan Livingston Seagull; Seth Speaks; Way of the Peaceful Warrior; Conversations with God; The Celestine Prophecy; Mutant Message Down Under; The Tibetan Book of Living and Dying; The Art of Happiness; Everything*

I Ever Needed to Know I Learned in Kindergarten. By the time I was a teenager, the wisdom machine was in full gear and showing no signs of stopping anytime soon. Coming of age in the heyday of America's love affair with wisdom-as-product, I was part of the first generation of confused teenagers to have this remarkable supermarket of both exotic and homespun insights glistening out there, ready to be of help to me if I wanted it.

And want it I did.

Whether their present popularity is judged as a good thing or a bad, wisdom books don't just promise to affect people's lives; they actually do so. I know this because of the way they have affected mine. My life has taken some of the odder turns it has because I discovered, and started avidly feeding on, this crop of wisdom material when I was a teenager. Like many others my age, I spent much of my near-adult life listening to a chorus of wise voices that told me with wonderfully appealing assurance what life is, how it got that way, and how to navigate it—voices that were not there in anything like the same variety for the generation before mine. Growing up at a moment when the wisdom coffers of ages past had been opened wider than they had ever been before, and when wisdom itself was being transformed into a product designed specifically for consumption, I developed what turned out to be an unquenchable appetite for it.

Anyone who read enough of the kind of books I read as a teenager noticed that there was a certain character who appeared in many of them: a person unlike other people. This person could be either a man or a woman, but let's say for the moment that he is a man. Things fall into place for this man in a way that they don't for others. Doors open and shut for him as if they had known just when he was coming. Trains and buses pull up when he wants them to. Even the weather changes to suit his needs—though, due to his extraordinary and inexplicable contentedness, those needs tend to be modest in the extreme. Unlike most people, who struggle and chafe against a world that is all too often at odds with their desires, this man seems to have struck up a secret agreement with life when no one was looking, and as a result events just seem to go his way. Wanting next to nothing, he receives everything.

For a while, I nurtured a private hope of actually bumping into one of these magical figures and learning from him first-hand instead of simply from the pages of a book. The way I imagined it, I would be going about my business on a day seemingly just like any other, when I would suddenly find myself face-to-face with him. Perhaps I would be in a bus sta-tion, like Carlos Castaneda was when he first met the Yaqui sorcerer don Juan Matus. Or perhaps, like the writers of some other narratives I'd read, I would be in a café, looking absently out the window, when I would notice a mysterious man at a table across from mine—and even though I had never seen him before, I would feel like I had known him all my life. Somehow we would get to talking, and this man would explain things to me that I had always wanted and needed to know, but that no one had ever offered to tell me before.

Not that I spent much time in either bus stations or cafés as a teenager, but that didn't matter because I knew this man could show up anywhere. The longer I waited to bump into this figure, the more important he grew to me. He became the absent center, the missing piece from the puzzle of my life. Once I found him, and once he had taught me the things I needed to know—the things I *really* needed to know, as opposed to what most of the adults around wanted to teach me—everything else would slide into place. Thanks to this encounter with a living embodiment of genuine, no-nonsense, transformatory wisdom with a capital *W,* my life, formerly so frustrating and formless and vague, would begin to make real sense at last.

I was predisposed to brood on this wonderful figure for a number of reasons, not the least of which being that I had one of them for a parent. Or rather, I was supposed to. Because my father was a celebrated figure in the emerging New Age movement, and because my knowledge of him was intimate enough to make me realize that he was in fact not the blemishless and all-knowing sage that his followers seemed to want him to be but rather simply another part-good-part-bad human being, the weight of faith I placed on my wisdom books, and the superhuman sagely figures who crowded their pages, was all the more intense. On the run from the conventional adulthood I feared life held in store for me, and largely distrustful of the noisy bohemianism at work in my father's circle, I was on the lookout for an entrance into a mysterious third path between these options, and a person who might genuinely be able to teach it to me.

Or if not an *actual* person, at least a continuing stream of good books featuring one.

Life Manuals are sacred literature for a culture that has forgotten what to do with its original sacred literature. They are books that offer recipes for living, but which typically do so without aggressive hucksterism. (Self-help books aren't Life Manuals, though sometimes the line is hard to draw.) Part of the charm and pull of Life Manuals is their refusal to promise that the whole wide world can benefit from their messages. Even when they sell in the millions, Life Manuals have a just-between-us quality and convey a message that has the flavor of a deep confidence whispered in one's ear. "Listen," these books seem to say, "don't spread this around too much, but here's the deal with life, what it's really all about, and what you can do to live it in a truly meaningful and genuine way." The suggestion is usually that the insights being offered are for the few, not the many: for people awake, alert, and alive enough to notice that ordinary life isn't quite what it should be, and that a solution to this problem exists for those hungry enough to find it. Even when it is as packed as an interstate on Labor Day weekend, the path of wisdom needs to feel like a side route, not the main artery.

Life Manuals are usually, though not always, short. *Zen and the Art of Motorcycle Maintenance*, one of the defining books of the genre—and, to my mind, one of the best—isn't slim at all; but by virtue of the fact that it offers a compelling, personal, no-nonsense recipe for making sense of life that has been seized upon and actively used by thousands of people, it passes my informal test. Life Manuals are books that are carried around long after one has finished reading them the first time, to be consulted again and again. As with cookbooks or bird-watching guides, the mark of their success is how dog-eared they become.

Life Manuals can come in the form of fiction or nonfiction (or poetry), and do not necessarily need to have been originally designed for such use by their authors. For example, a case could be made that J. D. Salinger's books—especially *Franny and Zooey* and *The Catcher in the Rye*—are Life Manuals, because they have been carried around and consulted as navigational life tools by countless people. Similarly, a number of Henry Miller's works—which make an appearance here in chapter 5—have become Life Manuals for some people, in spite of the fact that Miller himself might have had mixed feelings about this.

Just as some unlikely authors have ended up producing Life Manuals despite themselves, others lie outside the category in my eyes, even though they might seem to belong at its very center. For example, in spite of all the dog-eared copies of *The Road Less Traveled* out there in the world, and while psychologist M. Scott Peck writes with obvious power and insight on many of the topics discussed here, I somehow have difficulty thinking of him as a bona fide Life Manual author. (One reason for this is Peck's relentlessly honest insistence that he himself is just as flawed as the next fellow; he refuses to present himself as possessing anything special, wisdom-wise. This is not typical behavior for a Life Manual author: even the more humble ones tend to present themselves as speaking from a place above or apart from the norm.) Obviously there is no clear-cut definition of what does or doesn't make a book a Life Manual, but it is my hope that most people will not have much trouble understanding the kind of book I am talking about. Nor, I suspect, will the ideal of wisdom that these books point to in their various ways be unfamiliar to many.

Finally, it should be mentioned ahead of time that, with the brief exception of the discussion of Sophia in chapter 3, the Life Manual universe described in these pages is one in which Christianity scarcely shows up. This is in keeping with my experiences as a young consumer of Life Manual literature. For though He remains the primary archetype of wisdom in the West, Jesus, and the singularly specific and uncompromising program of transformation that he offered the world, were rarely presented to me for consideration by my wisdom authors except in the most passing, dismissive, and truncated fashion. This isn't surprising given that most of those authors were products of Christian culture themselves, and, for good reasons or bad, hard at work rebelling against that heritage.

It is precisely because I grew up in a place and time when the Bible had only recently ceased being *the* wisdom book and Jesus *the* model of transformatory wisdom (at least for a fair portion of the population) that the burst of imported or freshly invented contenders for these positions was able to occur in the first place. Yet for all that Jesus and Christianity are absent from the immediate proceedings, that absence is always something of a pregnant one. It could almost be said that the ideas and adventures described here unfolded within the space vacated by Christianity. Whether the space should ever have been vacated in the first place is a question I have chosen not to approach.

CHAPTER 1

THE TAO OF LIFE

A Small White Book on the Way of Life

Before everything, there was the Tao. Subtle and silent, void of all form or extension, and yet at the same time immeasurably vast, it held the noise and pandemonium of the entire universe within itself, like a mother awaiting term. It was from deep within the boundless watery hush of the Tao that the world and all the things within it were born, and once it had given birth to them, these things became like objects moving downstream in a giant river. In the river's great drift, nothing stays as it is for long. Trees, animals, entire civilizations: all of this material is like the scrim of twigs and litter you see flowing past on a day following a hard rain. Sometimes bobbing at the surface, sometimes sinking out of sight, drifting and bumping and turning in the dark, downward-moving water, all things flow in the Tao without knowing it. Beyond all thought and action, beyond both life and death, the Tao is the one constant, the sole aspect of all the universe that is entirely beyond change. It is the ultimate source, the ultimate support, and the ultimate destination of everything there is.

I first learned about the great Tao in the summer of 1979, when I was seventeen. I was on a canoe trip in the woods of northern Canada, and spending a good deal of my time amid the flowing water that plays such a big part in Taoist writings. I had signed on for this trip because it had seemed like it might satisfy a yearning that had been building in me recently: a desire to go on a journey that would help me make sense of who I was and what I was doing in the world. This particular journey, however, turned out to be a far more labor-intensive affair than I had expected, and I almost immediately found myself wishing that I was back home in my room, reading about adventures rather than actually being stuck in one. Books, and the time to read them, were luxury items on this trip. As the days wore on and my fellow campers and I slogged through mile after mile of muskeg and moss and paddled our canoes through one endless lake or river after another, sometimes even paddling *up* rivers for days on end, the moments I would have to myself, to think or read among the small collection of books I had brought with me, took on greater and greater importance.

As I struggled to find short moments of psychic sustenance within their covers, I soon realized that the selection of books I had made was not an ideal one. Awakening every day around five-thirty and traveling until the sun was touching the tops of the trees, I found myself placing a great burden of expectation on whatever I happened to be reading during the few stray minutes when I was both comfortable and awake enough to do so at all. What I needed was the literary equivalent of pemmican or beef jerky—something concentrated, pithy, and powerful—and the titles I had brought along just weren't doing the trick.

Growing ever more frustrated with my own little stack of

paperbacks, I began to eye the collection of one of my fellow campers. Like everyone else on the trip, this individual was some years older than I, but I saw that more than everyone else he seemed to know his literature. Central to his collection was a small, white, wafer-thin volume with a large Chinese character printed on the cover, and the words *The Way of Life* beneath. Tired, uncomfortable, itching from countless mosquito and black fly bites, and irritated at the outrageous amount of work that my wilderness adventure was demanding of me, I found the look of this little volume increasingly appealing. So there was an entire strategy for living that could fit into such a slim package? If there was, I wanted to know about it.

Back in civilization at the end of the summer, I hunted around in bookstores until I found a copy of the thin white volume and bought it. *The Way of Life According to Lao-tzu, An American Version* by Witter Bynner. I took the book home and commenced to study it in earnest.

The Disaster of Adulthood

On Saturday afternoons when I was a child, I often turned on a show called *The Wide World of Sports*. I had no great interest in watching, but the title sequence was irresistible to me. Each week, as a montage of assorted athletic events flashed across the screen, an announcer said something like the following: "Bringing you the entire world of sports in all its variety, from the thrill of victory . . . to the agony of defeat." As the announcer spoke the last part of this sentence—the "agony of defeat" part—a clip would run of a skier on a jump. Down the skier whizzed. Then, just as he got to the end of the jump and flew off into space, something went terribly wrong. Instead of jetting gracefully up into the air, the skier was transformed by some invisible error—some tiny miscalculation known, perhaps, only to him—into a hurtling ball of limbs. Crashing head-long through the barricades and banners, knocking object after object down, and refusing to stop no matter how many people and things he ran into, the unknown hero of this tragedy became a weekly reminder of just how wrong things could go in life if you weren't careful—and perhaps even if you were.

The agony of defeat was a topic I devoted quite a bit of thought to throughout my childhood, and by the time I was seventeen I had arrived at certain conclusions about it. From my perspective at this age, the real defeat to watch out for—the botched jump of all botched jumps, the disaster of all disasters—was nothing less than the condition of adulthood itself. For all the assorted benefits and privileges that came with it, all the evidence suggested that to become a grown-up was to lose a certain essential zest and spontaneity. If there was no way of avoiding adulthood altogether, wasn't there perhaps a better *kind* of adulthood to enter than the kind I saw around me?

That was where the Tao came in. Go to a bookstore today and you will find any number of Taos. The Tao of Business. The Tao of Tennis. The Tao of Pooh. The word *Tao* is both so inescapable and so threadbare these days that it is easy to forget that, just a few decades ago, it was a new—and extraordinary—addition to the American cultural vocabulary. A teenager in 1949, 1959, and probably even 1969 would most likely not have had the slightest idea about the Tao—neither that you pro-nounced it with a *D* and not a *T* sound nor that an understand-ing of it was the antidote to the hectic and contorted world of ordinary adult existence and all the ills that went along with it.

For a certain sort of teenager—and in 1979 I was definitely this sort—learning about the Tao was like reinstating a missing vitamin into my diet, one that no one had told me I needed before, but whose absence had secretly created all sorts of dis-comforts and deficiencies. Thanks to the Tao—and specifically,

Lao-tzu's little book outlining what it was all about—I was given a genuinely useful tool for making sense of the countless yeses and noes, the endless arbitrary goods and bads, of which my life was full: SATs, B-pluses, C-minuses, physics, chemistry, biology, biochemistry, college placement, wisdom teeth, sexual frustration, driver's ed. . . . In the midst of all this garbage, the Tao descended upon my imaginative life like a magic lens, allowing me to see it for what it really was. For the Tao was, quite simply, bigger than all this stuff. Bigger, and yet at the same time so subtle and simple that when you tried to describe it, to imprison it in some sort of categorical box, you ended up with nothing.

From the beginning of time, translator Bynner assured me, the Tao had possessed this marvelous simplicity. And likewise from the beginning, people had been out to mess with it—to dress the Tao up as something it wasn't and spoil all the good that came from just allowing it to take its mysterious course. The history of the Tao was, in fact, little more than a list of the endless attempts by confounders and complicators of one sort or another to distort the words of the ancient masters who had lived in effortless harmony with it. The great project for someone like me, then, who had not yet calcified into one of these Tao-obstructing adults, was to somehow learn how to get in line with the Tao before that happened.

The question was how to do it. According to legend, old Lao-tzu himself—if he had in fact ever existed, for this was open to question—ultimately got so fed up with his fellow humans' inability to follow the Tao that he had only scribbled the eighty-one chapters of the *Tao-te Ching* down at the behest of a gatekeeper whom he passed while leaving civilization once and for all on the back of a water buffalo. Even in the mists of China two thousand and some years ago, the chances of growing into one of these supple, Tao-attuned adults was slim. What chance would I have, marooned in the suburbs of late-twentieth-century America?

The Adult Unlike Other Adults

The multitude of men look satisfied and pleased. . . . I alone seem listless and still, my desires having as yet given no indication of their presence. I am like an infant which has not yet smiled.

—TAO-TE CHING

The *Tao-te Ching* is in many ways the original wisdom book, by the original Adult Unlike Other Adults. The figure of Lao-tzu, or The Old Boy, as this name is sometimes translated, has a basic vagueness to it that is profoundly satisfying, and the fact that Lao-tzu might not have existed at all only furthers his charm. Lao-tzu lives at such a distance from us that he serves as an ideal canvas—rough, bright, absorbent—for the wild brush strokes of our creative projections of the perfect adult. The same holds for his little book on the Way of Life, which legend tells us Lao-tzu knocked off in three days after that gatekeeper he passed on his way into the mists of history requested it from him. The *Tao-te Ching's* text is so relentlessly ambiguous that some scholars have argued that not a single statement within it can be interpreted in one way only. This Rorschach quality has made the *Tao-te Ching* perhaps the most durable wisdom book around.

Tao literally means "path" or "way," and from Lao-tzu, hovering at the flickering fringes of existence and legend, comes one of the very first recorded emphases on the image of a path or way that one deliberately walks through life, as well as the notion that this path is set distinctly apart from the one the majority of humans are trudging. Also from Lao-tzu comes one of the first statements of the basic wisdom book idea that most people, deny it though they might, aren't really happy. An ingredient that nobody talks about but everybody, at some level of his or her mind, is thinking about all the same, is missing. Since the *Tao-te Ching* first pointed this fact out, people have never tired of hearing it.

Upon completing my grueling and inconclusive wilderness adventure, I returned to my room on the second floor of my sister and brother-in-law's house in the suburbs of Virginia just outside Washington. I had moved from my parents' to my sister's house the previous year—ostensibly because she lived closer to the Washington high school I was now attending, but also to take a vacation of sorts from my parents' world. Unlike my bohemian father and mother, my sister and brother-in-law were "normal," and this quality had come as something of a relief when I joined their household.

Not that I wanted to *be* like my sister or my brother-in-law—admirable folk as they were in many ways—any more than I wanted to be like my parents. To me at seventeen, normalcy and rebellion were both little more than two sides of the same useless coin. The trick, as I saw it, was to become one of that magical third group, whose members neither railed against the regular world around them nor made up a part of it. These were the invisible ones: the ones who drifted through life somewhere far above the rest, in the pull of a larger, more meaningful current. The people of the Tao.

Mud

The skillful masters of the Tao in old times, with a subtle and exquisite penetration, comprehended its mysteries. . . . Evanescent like ice that is melting away; unpretentious like wood that has not been fashioned into anything; vacant like a valley, and dull like muddy water.

—TAO-TE CHING

Anticipating the chaos theorists who now tell us more or less the same thing in different terms, the Taoists maintained that the entire universe was characterized by flux. Everything is in a constant state of destruction and reconstruction, with one thing transforming into another, one thing devouring another, in an endless orgy of ingestion, defecation, germination, combustion, disintegration, and procreation.

Rather than recoiling in horror at the sight of this universe where nothing sits still and nothing is safe from ultimate destruction—as the Buddha and his followers were to do over in India—the early Taoists claimed to be completely at home in it. Wandering here and there in the pull of the great Tao, changing their habits along with the seasons, these men lived out their lives to the fullest; and when it came time to die, they did that well, too. "These great Taoists," scholar Herlee G. Creel writes, "were so thrilled by the fact that they were inalienably a part of this mighty cosmos that the incident of death seemed quite insignificant." When death arrived, we are told, they fell apart like gingerbread men, smiling to the last.

So enthusiastic were the ancient Taoists about the transformations and destructions taking place in the universe around them that dirt and mud—the symbols par excellence of the final destination of all things, no matter how ordered and lofty—are rivaled only by water as the natural substance they called upon to illustrate their view of life. In the *Chuang-tzu*, the celebrated book of Chinese wisdom that is second only to the *Tao-te Ching* as a source of Taoist ideas, the universe itself is called the "Great Clod" (in Burton Watson's translation), or the "Mighty Mudball" (in David Hinton's).

The Taoist concept that brings out this mudlike aspect of the universe more than any other is Hun Tun—a word sometimes translated as "dark essence" or, simply, "chaos." All things, at heart, are Hun Tun, and all things are destined, ultimately, to return to it. Like so much of Taoism, Hun Tun is not really susceptible to any single definition, but most of its translations hint at the idea of a certain ungraspable mixed-up-ness that lies at the heart of all phenomenal existence. As Toshihiko Izutsu, one of Taoism's most respected scholars, has described it, Hun Tun means "an amorphous state where nothing is clearly delineated, nothing is clearly distinguishable, but which is far from being sheer non-being; it is, on the contrary, an extremely obscure 'presence' in which the existence of something—or some things, still undifferentiated—is vaguely and dimly sensed."

In the seventh chapter of the *Chuang-tzu*, the story is told of a certain emperor of a shadowy land lying between the North Sea, ruled by the Emperor Hu, and the South Sea, ruled by the Emperor Shu. This emperor's name was Hun Tun. Hu and Shu once paid a visit to the domain of Hun Tun, who was distinguished by having none of the seven bodily openings normally present in human beings. At the end of their stay, Hu and Shu were so impressed with their host's hospitality that they resolved to do him a favor. Taking hold of Hun Tun, they carefully drilled seven holes where body openings would have been on an ordinary human. They drilled a new opening each day "until the seventh day," when, as the text of the *Chuang-tzu* laconically states, "Hun Tun died."

Just because all things belong at their core to the chaos of Hun Tun does not mean that it is open to inspection or manipulation. This, it has been argued, is the meaning of Chuang-tzu's story of Hu and Shu and their ill-fated visit with the emperor. The minute you try to lay a finger on it, the story suggests—the minute you try to bring Hun Tun into the light for all to see and understand—this magical, shadowy chaos will die on you, and you will be no wiser than when you began.

Hun Tun is darkness, chaos, and mystery. It is the truth of

life in its ungraspable and invisible essence—seemingly susceptible to manipulation at one moment, yet ready to slip through
one's fingers and vanish at the next. It is the wild flux of creation, and of destruction as well, and just as it is resistant to
being grasped and held when one goes in search of it, so, too,
is it ultimately impossible to resist when it, instead, goes in
search of us.

Voices of Hun Tun

As the weeks passed, the influence of Lao-tzu's words upon me,
and those of other writers on the Tao that I started to come
across, grew and grew. Like a river in flood season overflowing
its banks and obscuring the lines of the countryside around it,
the great Tao, and the books I read about it, slowly but surely
swallowed up all my other interests and concerns. History, science, English: like houses shuddering on their foundations,
their basements filling up with roiling brown water until their
walls finally gave way and drifted off downstream, all rival concerns ultimately surrendered to the Tao's relentless pull.

Perhaps it was only appropriate that I should have ended up
enlisting the sponsorship of the Tao as enthusiastically as I did,
for the Tao's and my histories were intertwined from the very
beginning. I was born in 1962, right around the time when the
Tao as a going concern was getting its first real foothold in
America. In California in 1962 Eastern mysticism was much on
people's minds, and had been increasingly so ever since the
May morning nine years earlier when Aldous Huxley had
flushed out the doors of his perception with a glass of water
and dissolved mescaline powder and written about the experiences that followed. Huxley and his circle (most notably Gerald Heard and Christopher Isherwood) had been popularizing
Indian mysticism with increasing effect in the Los Angeles

area, and in the northern part of the state the same thing was happening with the Chinese and Japanese varieties. The chief voice on behalf of these latter traditions was that of another British émigré—a recently resigned Episcopal priest named Alan Watts. In the early fifties, following a messy departure from a clergy post at the University of Chicago, the captivating, eloquent, and personable Watts had set up shop in the San Francisco area—and it was he who really got the word out on what Americans, and especially young Americans, could learn from Taoism, Zen Buddhism, and other Far Eastern traditions.

Watts was the great master of pop mystical rhetoric, the most energetic and influential among the creators of that whole body of what-to-do-about-life literature that started to appear in force in America in the early sixties. If you went looking for news of the Tao in the seventies, Watts was still the first, and the friendliest, voice you were likely to come across. I discovered Watts early on in my Taoistic investigations, and did my best to put his prescriptions for becoming one with the Tao (or rather for realizing my inherent unity with it, for the first thing you learned from Watts was that there was no getting away from the Tao even if you wanted to) into action.

Watts's great desire was to undermine Western civilization's infatuation with structure—to get people away from Hu and Shu and back into the far more satisfactory domain of Emperor Hun Tun. According to Watts, the universe was a squiggly and structure-free place: a vast, playful arena where distinctions of up and down, right and left, and even good and evil ultimately meant nothing. From acne to Auschwitz, the negative stuff that life had to offer only seemed to possess a solid ontological core. Worrying too much about categories like Good and Bad was, Watts reported, like making "comparisons between right and wrong stars . . . between well and badly arranged constellations." From the perspective of one who sees things from the *inside* of the Tao—rather than from the outside, where most poor saps thought they were stuck—life unfolds "beyond anxiety."

"If we live, we live," said Watts, apparently speaking directly from the very heart of Hun Tun's domain. "If we die, we die; if we suffer, we suffer; if we are terrified, we are terrified. There is no problem about it."

Watts was also very interested in dispossessing people of their mistaken notions of self. "The ego," he assured his readers, "is neither a spiritual, psychological, or biological reality but a social institution of the same order as the monogamous family, the calendar, the clock, the metric system, and the agreement to drive on the right side of the road." With a little effort on my part—or rather the right kind of noneffort from my self that was in truth a nonself—I would, Watts told me, find my way into a condition where that problematic, embarrassing, anxiety-prone fiction I called *me* would be mercifully left behind. In its place there would appear "a continuous, self-moving stream of experiencing, without the sense either of an active subject who controls it or of a passive subject who suffers it. The thinker would be seen to be no more than the series of thoughts, and the feeler no more than the feelings." In other words, I would become the Tao and the Tao would become me.

Sinking into the Mud

It doesn't take a confirmed Taoist to understand that life is confusing—that everything in it is mixed up with everything else, to the point where distinguishing one aspect from another with any consistency is all but impossible. Good people act bad at some times, bad people act good at others. It's a mess. The people who write wisdom books know this, of course, and tend to counter this problem by dividing up their work into neat, clean compartments. Once again, the *Tao-te Ching* sets the precedent. Life may have been a chaotic stew of endless transformation and destruction for the ancient Taoists, but open any of the dozens of English translations of the *Tao-te Ching* that appeared in the twentieth century and your eyes fall upon pure order and clarity. Eighty-one chapters, all full of calm, clean, declarative sentences like "Those who know do not say," and "The way to do is to be."

To read the *Tao-te Ching*, like most effective Life Manuals, is to be pulled away for a moment from the swamp of ordinary events and into a wonderful new domain where things actually do seem to be making more sense than usual. "Maybe now," many can't help thinking when encountering this book for the first time, "I'm going to get to the bottom of things at last." Yet for all their reassuring beauty on the page, there is something about the proclamations of these mighty mudball masters that is challenging, and even slightly chilling, to the reader who tries to take them seriously. I encountered this chilly aspect of the Taoist project early on in my investigations, and for a long time I didn't know how to make my peace with it.

Part of my reservations about fully immersing myself in Lao-tzu's water and Chuang-tzu's mud no doubt had to do with my particular, personal associations with the latter of these two substances. As a child I lived near a large lake that in summertime functioned as a public swimming area. Two wooden platforms, held up by a series of metal drums, floated at anchor out in the lake's center and were matched on shore by a pair of long narrow docks with a stretch of trucked-in white sand lying between them. The lake was shallow and swampy in parts, and swimmers tended to stay in the deep water right around the two floating platforms. Children were encouraged to keep to the sandy area and not to step into the water on the far side of either dock, for if you did your foot sank into a layer of black, ultrafine mud that a few inches down turned into a thick bed of clay. The mud and clay sucked at your feet, making walking difficult and uncomfortable.

One day when I was ten or so I watched a boy about my age march out into this muddy area on the far side of one of the docks. Taking one step after another, the boy left a rich black trail in the water behind him. After several of these bold, deep steps, he stopped short, uttered a little bark of surprise, and limped back out onto dry land. One of the adults on hand came over and held his foot up to examine it. A slick of blood, bright like enamel model paint, flowed from the upheld foot and blended with the mud and clay that coated the pale skin of the boy's leg. Apparently he had made contact with a buried edge of some sort—a broken bottle or the torn lip of a tin can—and it had cut deep into his big toe. All that blood mixing with the mud and clay had a shiny, voluptuous look to it, and I could imagine what it must have felt like as the hidden object cut into the toe—so fast and clean and decisive that at first the boy would not have known that something had broken the skin at all.

For me at age seventeen, groping my way into the curiously tranquil teachings of my new Taoist masters, there was a lingering suspicion that the mighty mudball of the world held a little more than what they said it did: something alien and sinister, and not so easy to love as all that. It was one thing, it seemed to me, to happily contemplate one's disintegration into a universe composed solely of the floating clouds, flowing rivers, and whispering trees in which Lao-tzu, Chuang-tzu, and their associates had presumably made their home. But what about the universe I had been born into—the one of napalm, lead-based paint, child molesters, and fifteen-car pileups? Was sinking into the mud of Hun Tun really as viable a business in my day as it had been for the Taoists in theirs?

Mind at Large

Despite these initial doubts and perplexities, my research into the alternate life to which my new wisdom masters had alerted me continued to move forward. From Watts's assured proclamations on how to make oneself at home with the disorder of the universe, I soon made my way to Huxley and found that he was full of no less heady and promising stuff. The edition of *The Doors of Perception* I purchased at a local shopping mall that fall cost me ninety-five cents plus tax and weighed in at an astonishing sixty-seven pages. The book was no fatter than my copy of the *Tao-te Ching*, and in that very smallness I read portent: clearly another crucial manual for living had come my way.

A scant six or seven pages in, Huxley, having drunk his famous half-glass of mescaline-laced water, was "seeing what Adam had seen on the morning of his creation . . . a bunch of flowers shining with their own inner light and all but quivering under the pressure of the significance with which they were charged." This significance, in turn, was made up of "nothing more, and nothing less, than what they were—a transience that was yet eternal life, a perpetual perishing that was at the same time pure Being, a bundle of minute, unique particulars in which, by some unspeakable and yet self-evident paradox, was to be seen the divine source of all existence."

For page after page, as Huxley wandered back and forth between his living room and garden, looking at pictures of paintings in books, listening to music, and staring for minutes on end at a garden chair or his pants leg, I followed along as if my life depended on it. *The Doors of Perception* was less a book than a telegram, sent from the high peaks of essential insight down into the foggy flatlands of ordinary consciousness where I was for the moment—but only for the moment—stuck.

According to Huxley, the mind had what he called a "reducing valve"—the product of its evolution in the harsh realities of day-to-day survival—and that it acted automatically to filter out all the fabulous, super-luminescent suchness of the world as it truly was, leaving instead the bleached, boring, and all-too-ordinary one that I was more than used to. It was this reducing valve which accounted for the readily observable fact that so many of the adults around me appeared to be having such a dull time in life. If turning into an adult was exactly the disaster I had started to suspect it to be, Huxley was actually giving me some genuine, nuts-and-bolts hints on how to avoid this fate myself.

The blast of clarity Huxley had attained with his half-glass of mescaline was, I was happy to read, potentially available to anyone—with drugs but preferably without. Mescaline was nothing magical or mystical in itself. It simply had the effect of reducing the supply of sugar fed to the brain, thus allowing what Huxley tantalizingly referred to as "Mind at Large" to flow past the gates of the ordinarily circumscribed ego (the same ego that, thanks to Watts, I already knew didn't really exist anyhow). The basic trouble in life was that ordinary adults had been conditioned by the necessities of the workaday world to shut themselves off from this domain. Caught up in the struggle for survival, we had all trained ourselves to say No to the greater reality, even though the splendors of Mind at Large were all around, just waiting for us to take notice of them.

"For the artist as for the mescaline taker," Huxley confided as I lay in my bed on the second floor of my sister's house late one night, "draperies are living hieroglyphs that stand in some peculiarly expressive way for the unfathomable mystery of pure being." Looking up from the book, I could see that the draperies hanging in *my* room certainly weren't any of these things—but that was all right for the moment because now I at least knew they could be.

Patterns of Organic Energy

By the time I got to them in that fall of 1979, the proclamations of Huxley and Watts on the Tao, Hun Tun, mescaline, enlightenment, Mind at Large, and related matters were no longer hot from the oven but cool and crusty with age. Both men were dead by this point, and over the last decade and a half or so, legions of other disgruntled seventeen-year-olds had already seized upon their books as road maps to a different and better sort of life. But I didn't know this at the time and might not have cared if I did. After all, if others before me had had the maps but failed to find the treasure, that was not necessarily the fault of the maps.

So I read on. Like a child wandering along the beach after a great storm, picking up interesting pieces of flotsam that the waters have blown up onto the sand, I went from paperback to paperback, from voice to confident, reassuring, visionary voice, growing more convinced with each one I discovered that a genuine plan of action could be found: a way out of the disappointingly ordinary—or in the case of my father, obnoxiously extraordinary—adulthood that I knew was coming.

My knowledge of the Tao grew ever more eclectic. Huxley's mescaline narratives and Watts's sermons on Hun Tun were soon joined by the explicators of the mesons, gluons, quarks, and subquarks of the new physics. Zipping in and out of existence, transforming into each other, moving forward and backward in time, these likable subatomic entities, it turned out, actually made up the stuff of the entire world around me. More than one writer informed me that the very table I was reading at was something in the neighborhood of 99.999999 percent empty space. Not only that, but the less than .000001 percent of the table that was "matter" was itself nothing more than a temporary knot of energy. And energy, my authors were quick to mention, was at bottom just a particularly congealed and intractable form of consciousness itself. I was the table, and the table was me.

My vocabulary grew along with my reading list. I learned about *Wu-Wei*, or doing-nondoing, the mysterious method of active nonaction that the Taoist masters of old had employed on those rare occasions when they actually needed to get something done in the world. I learned as well about *Wu Li*, or "patterns of organic energy"—a term that described all the random-yet-intelligent shapes that appear in nature, from the formations made by migrating birds, to the tracings left by breaking waves along a beach, to the routes (both forward and backward in time) followed by the subatomic particles in the table I was reading at. And I tried, in my haphazard teenage manner, to apply the whole mass of this material to my daily life. During study period at school, I practiced "sitting in oblivion," the ancient Taoist technique of allowing one's mind to become empty so that only the pure white static of the universe would flow through it, like the snow on a television screen after all the programs are off the air. Doing the dishes after dinner with my sister and brother-in-law, I would ponder again and again Watts's admonitions, borrowed from the masters of old and slightly reformulated, to *be* the dishes—to surrender to the revolutionary assertion that, at bottom, dish and self were not different but one and the same.

Sometime before Christmas vacation, the select company of Oriental sages and nuclear physicists lining the little bookshelf by my bed was joined by the works of another great figure of the teenage transformatory wisdom manual: Carlos Castaneda. Don Juan, the squinty-eyed hero of Castaneda's celebrated odyssey in the deserts of Mexico and the American Southwest, dumped a whole new glossary of terms into my head. These all sounded strange at first, but before long they became as pleasantly familiar as *Wu-Wei, Wu Li,* and *Yin-Yang.* Following along behind the wise and wiry don Juan and the bumbling, hopelessly empirical Carlos, I journeyed into the otherworldly sands of the Sonora in search of the separate reality of the sorcerer's understanding. Along with thousands of other gratefully mystified teenagers hidden away in their own bedrooms across America, I learned about the luminous egg that humans look like to the eyes of a sorcerer, about getting spun by the Ally, about the difference between *seeing* and mere looking, and about making friends with my death. I learned that most human beings were stuck in the *tonal*—Castaneda's term for the ordinary, everyday world and the ordinary, everyday sort of consciousness that went along with it. And I nodded with satisfaction as don Juan explained to Carlos that this ordinary world that seemed to be all and everything was really only a little island, at the shores of which lapped the uncanny waters of the *nagual*—the place where draperies glowed like living hieroglyphs, flower vases became pulsating matrices of Buddha-like suchness, anthropology students flew like crows, and people turned into the giant luminous eggs that they had, in fact, been all along.

With varying degrees of success, I attempted to synthesize Carlos and don Juan's chilly, neo-Gnostic calisthenics out in the desert with what Alan and Aldous had told me about the nonexistence of my ego and my identity with the cosmos; and when I had these materials balanced together in my head for a moment, I threw in what I now knew about Bell's theorem, Planck's constant, and Heisenberg's uncertainty principle.

And on better days, when all this material did actually balance itself in my head for a moment or two, I felt what I had been so hoping to feel: that the Taoists and the Buddhists and the physicists and don Juan the Yaqui sorcerer were all talking about the same thing: a whole alternate universe, far more interesting than the one I was being groomed to inhabit by "consensus culture." Out beyond the shores of the *tonal*, the *nagual*—or the great Tao, or Mind at Large, or whatever you wanted to call it—lay, just waiting for me to plunge in.

Leaving the House

Wisdom books come in two basic varieties: those with plots and those without. Wisdom books without plots tend to be, like the *Tao-te Ching*, simple instruction books: recipes for living. Wisdom books with plots offer recipes for living, too, but these are folded into story lines, and these story lines tend to run in a very similar manner. There is the period of wandering, during which the hero seems to be drifting at the mercy of blind chance. Then, out of nowhere, there is the meeting with the master, the Adult Unlike Other Adults, who, after initially denying his role of teacher, submits the hero to a period of apprenticeship. During this period, the hero undergoes a series of trials, temptations, and confusions that are generally unpleasant but have the effect of gradually jolting him into higher levels of awareness. Finally, the moment arrives when enlightenment is reached, and the hero sets off happily on his own. Perhaps he will see the master again and perhaps he won't, but it doesn't really matter either way because he now possesses the secret to life himself. With that secret under his belt, he is ready to engage the world with the same ease, assurance, and power that the master himself had so impressively exhibited to him.

If wisdom books came in these two basic varieties, it seemed possible that people's lives might do so as well. If they did, which sort of life should I shoot for?

No matter how good my prospects for wisdom getting were starting to look during my late-night reading, out in the left-brain, Newtonian world I was still a high school senior, and because of this my attention was dragged away from my extracurricular studies with annoying regularity. Should I go to college? If so, which one? Thanks to all my reading on the Tao and its obfuscators, these questions tended to put me on the defensive. What, I explained to Mr. King, my ever-patient admissions counselor at school, could I expect to learn in an institution of higher learning that was going to take me anywhere but further away from that mysterious, neither-this-nor-that condition that constituted the true state of a man of the Tao? Even if I did go to college, what on earth would I study there? I could just imagine what Eastern Religion 105 would be like. Textbooks on the Tao! A total sacrilege.

Likewise, if I were to pursue an education in my own cultural legacy, the prospects were even uglier. The Iliad, The Odyssey, Moby Dick, Hamlet: much of the basic meat and potatoes of Western literature—material that I had successfully eluded so far—loomed before me like a great gray cloud of knockout dust. What did all these books amount to, really, but a long and ugly footnote to that initial subject-object dualism that, my new masters told me, had been initiated by the Greco-Roman, Judeo-Christian worldview some twenty-five hundred years ago? As for the science courses with which I would no doubt be threatened, these would only poison my understanding further.

Who needed any of it? Why not avoid contamination by this sort of thinking altogether and simply hang out, instead, with my select library of Taoists, Zen masters, and Yaqui metaphysicians? How was *Moby Dick* ever going to help me do those blasted dishes with the right attitude? For when all was said and done, it was precisely things like doing the dishes— and all the other ordinary, inexplicable little chores and obligations that filled my life—that were the real problem. How was I to steer between the Scylla of an ordinary life and the Charybdis of an extraordinary one? How was I to stick to the true path and become the Taoist Nobody that I really aspired to be?

As the year ground on, I sat through the majority of my school classes with the attitude of a miner forced by an uncaring coal company to work a defunct vein. As soon as possible, I was going to toss all the straw of Western learning aside once and for all and take a big bite of Huxleyan visionary bread. I needed to figure out how to open up the flow nozzle of Mind at Large, to shift from a habitual into a nonhabitual mode of perception, to subvert the tyranny of the known and recover the incalculably greater realities of the hidden-yet-unhidden Tao. From here on out, I knew, it would just be a matter of time until I did so.

CHAPTER 2

THE YOGA OF ACTION

In the Bowels of the Western Behemoth

When we renounce learning we have no troubles.

—TAO-TE CHING

The next fall, for lack of anything else to do, I went off to Vassar College, my head still full of forebodings about all the ways in which the faculty there would be attempting to subvert what small understanding of the unwalkable Way I had thus far achieved. The place was pleasant enough to look at, and I had based my choice of it almost entirely on this. Huge trees grew up among a maze of heavyset brick buildings, many of them covered with matrices of dense, dark ivy. Vassar had until recently been an all-women's college, and I had got the idea that its lingering sissy image might be evidence of a greater openness to that Tao-attuned side of life that I was looking to cultivate. Western consciousness being a patriarchal affair, wouldn't a women's college stand a better chance of being outfitted with the sort of yin energy needed to combat it?

Unfortunately, this assumption proved to be off the mark. I was barely settled in my single room on the third floor of one of those ivy-covered structures before it became obvious that, sissy image or not, the place was a hotbed of entrenched Western thought patterns. In each imposing building, in every plaque proclaiming when and in honor of whom this or that structure was erected, in every measured walkway, and behind every last leaf of all that dense green ivy, I began to detect the hulking, sinister presence of the Western tradition: the materialistic, rationalistic, Tao-denying behemoth that I had vowed to evade in my journey to genuine adulthood.

A History Lesson

Most Life Manuals with a historical focus will tell you that the modern world's problems really got started with the Scientific Revolution. In the sixteenth century, Nicolaus Copernicus knocked the earth out of its long-held spot at the center of the universe, and in so doing paved the way for scientific relativism. Unlike Taoist relativism, which somehow managed to downplay the centrality and importance of human beings without painting a depressing picture of things, scientific relativism was a grim business indeed, and basically had the effect of taking all the joy out of life. Shortly after Copernicus shattered the old geocentric picture of the universe and transformed the earth from the centerpiece of creation into an unimportant pebble at its periphery, Galileo looked up at the new, relativistic skies and began measuring the movements of the stars and planets moving across it with an astonishing accuracy. The scientific laws he found at work in the heavens were soon brought down to the surface of the earth, and suddenly everything upon it became susceptible to a new and unprecedentedly dispassionate style of perception. Where

Quality had long reigned, Quantity now took over, and a frenzy of measurement was loosed upon the world. The Judeo-Christian way of things had been problematic enough already, what with its harsh, dualistic, and decidedly un-Taoistic notions of sin and salvation, good and evil, and other such black-and-white subjects. But compared with what was happening now, all that stuff had been a picnic. Virtually overnight, Length, Weight, and Velocity replaced Truth, Beauty, and Goodness as the quarry to be hunted. The flavor had gone out of the world.

But the process was only just beginning. In England in the early seventeenth century, Francis Bacon further developed the newly discovered methods of taking the world's measure, along with the cold-blooded new attitudes that went along with them. Nature's secrets, according to Bacon, were now to be ruthlessly bullied out of her instead of respectfully coaxed, and no corner of the universe was to be left unransacked. Soon thereafter René Descartes arrived on the scene, with Sir Isaac Newton close on his heels, and between the two of them the final steps were taken in the process of downgrading the living cosmos into a vast impersonal machine, replete with endless moving parts and lots of immutable laws but absolutely nothing in the way of consciousness, meaning, or mystery. These latter qualities Descartes attributed to the thinking human subject, the *Cogito* of his famous *Cogito, ergo sum*, which scattered these purely subjective notions out onto the cold, hard linoleum of the world in the vain hope that they would stick. A hundred years further down the line, in the mid-nineteenth century, Darwin trivialized humankind's place in cosmic history much as Copernicus had trivialized its place in cosmic geography, showing that all of earth's species, including Homo sapiens, were the products of a long, blind, pointless process called natural selection, in which one randomly composed mass of protoplasm competed ruthlessly with other masses of protoplasm for the opportunity to feed and procreate.

Once shrunk down into the precarious and indeterminate container of the Cartesian subject, it was only a matter of time before the human personality was robbed of all its remaining pretenses to any sort of beauty or nobility. Immanuel Kant took great pains to demonstrate philosophically that genuine knowledge of anything in the outside world was an impossibility for any human being. The self or "I" of each person now became a hopelessly isolated epiphenomenon stuck amid a vast clockwork universe in which it played no role of any real and lasting importance, and with which it stood no chance of achieving any kind of cosmic oneness of the sort that Watts and the Taoists described. Freud capped this process off by denying the human "I" even the consolation of being in charge of itself. Caught up in the horrid cause-and-effect, kill-or-be-killed pinball machine of the Cartesian-Newtonian-Darwinian universe, the Ego, as Freud now christened it, turned out to be a mere pawn of the animalistic Id, which whispered its horrible instructions in secret and punished the Ego mercilessly when it disobeyed.

Get While the Getting Is Good

These bleak assertions bred deep consequences in the world of human conduct. The universe, once deprived of such presumably subjective qualities as beauty, nobility, and goodness, was ripe for the plundering, while the self—its cold Freudian hardwiring now exposed for all to see—was absolved of all responsibility for its crimes. Even before the last vestiges of the Judeo-Christian worldview had vanished down the gullet of scientific atheism, Western civilization had often been treating nature poorly enough thanks to the biblical emphasis on the primacy of humankind and the fallen status of all natural creation. But as Christian idealism succumbed to the cult of material progress and the capitalist imperative, the sins of the old Judeo-Christian patriarchy against nature began to look mild indeed. Fed by a lust for material gain and a deluded faith in endless material betterment, Western man set out upon the world with unprecedented rapacity. The forests and oceans were emptied of animals, native populations were demolished or forced into slavery, the dark satanic metropolises sprang up, and the way was paved for life in the wasteland of the modern world—a world where nature was in its death throes, materialism had eroded all sense of any larger meaning and purpose, and the isolated human subjectivity drifted like a ghost through a vast, plundered landscape from which all subtlety and magic had been squeezed like juice from a lemon.

No Time for Pessimism

Nobody can practice the yoga of action who is anxious about his future.

—BHAGAVAD GITA

So it was that things had got to the sorry pass they were at now. But—fortunately—the story did not end there. In fact, according to some, it was just beginning. Caught up in the wheels of the Western juggernaut, trapped in a world of dead matter and cold surfaces, it seemed from one angle that all hope for modern man was lost. But, as writers like Frithjof Capra and Gary Zukav were quick to explain, that was only how it looked from one angle. For right now, at this wretchedly low pass of history, something called a paradigm shift was under way. Entrenched though it might still be, the glory days of the Copernican-Cartesian-Newtonian picture had come and gone, and a new perception of the world was emerging in its place.

This new paradigm, which like a corn kernel lying long in the skillet was ready to pop into fulfillment at any moment, combined the best aspects of the old, prescientific world pictures with the most useful insights of modern science—especially quantum mechanics and relativity theory. In this new picture time and space were to be exposed as the tiresome illusions they had in fact always been. The seemingly solid world that post-Cartesian humankind had been clunking about in for the past four hundred years would transform into a swirling, magical confection of quarks and probabilities. Bell's theorem, which explained how space didn't really exist and all objects were in fact intimately connected with each other, would become a matter of common knowledge and experience. Pull one thread on the great carpet of the universe, everyone would soon realize, and all the others responded instantaneously. Likewise, the equally tiresome illusion of temporal duration—of an endless past and an uncertain future sandwiching the feeble meat of the present into near-nothingness—would be tossed in the trash bin too. These erroneous and threadbare conceptions would give way to a vision in which self and other, past and present, and all the other myriad dualisms of the old paradigm would lose their power and vanish. All would be seen to be one, just as it had been all along, and as my assorted masters of wisdom had been trying to tell everyone for centuries.

But, of course, none of this had happened just yet. The wreckage of the old world picture still lay all about, very much alive for all that it might be fatally wounded. In fact, as far as my particular life and the things that might be expected of me in it were concerned, it was as alive as it had ever been. This had already been thoroughly driven home for me long before I arrived at college. After all, had Mr. Caiola, my chemistry teacher back in high school, been interested in the fact that spatial distance and solid matter were illusions, that electrons, when making the leap from one valence to another, actually stopped existing altogether for a moment? Well, sort of. But not in the weirdly desperate way that I was. If I was going to genuinely profit from the breakdown of the modern Western worldview and the emergence of the new holistic metapicture, it was clear that I needed to keep far enough away from the clutches of the old paradigm to prevent it from poisoning me by contact. I needed to thread my way among the hissing, huffing, burned-out ideological beasts of the old worldview without allowing them to suck me in—to bide my time carefully as I waited for the kernel of the new vision to burst.

And right off the bat, college was looking like a place where this would be a tricky thing indeed to accomplish. That summer I had received a catalog of fall course offerings, which I now opened and studied seriously for the first time. To my distress, I found it positively brimming with Cartesian fare. Five courses needed to be chosen, to lead, eventually, to a major. As the unsavory look of all the courses, and the realization that like it or not I would really have to choose five of them, sank in, I considered bailing out completely. The problem was that my father had already signed a check for fall tuition, and I knew that at this late date none of that money would be refundable. I had a room of my own, a laminated three-meal-a-day card with my puzzled face emblazoned on it, and—as usual—no other concrete ideas about what to do with myself. So, reservations or not, I decided to stay.

No Matter How Much It May Not Seem That Way, You're Always Exactly Where You're Supposed to Be

What is action? What is inaction? Even the wise are puzzled by this question.

—BHAGAVAD GITA

As Jon Kabat-Zinn's recent best-selling Life Manual of the same name has put it, "wherever you go there you are." This classic notion that things are working out just as they are supposed to even when it seems like they aren't has been around for a long, long time—just as all of the other basic Life Manual insights have. The Greeks and the Jews may now and then have lapsed into fist shaking at the frustrating way that things down on the plain of earth tend to unfold, but over in the East, the practice of not only making do with the flawed nature of events but openly embracing them has long been recommended by the spiritually advanced. In China, Lao-tzu had much to say about the foolishness of struggling against one's situation in life, as did Chuang-tzu after him. But perhaps no country's wisdom traditions have argued the importance of saying yes to life, even when everything in it stinks, as persuasively as have India's.

Indian wisdom tends to see a person's position in life as the result of his or her karmic profile, built up both in their current incarnation and in the countless ones that have preceded it. Thanks in part to this deep and abiding belief in the laws of karma, Indian sages—be they Hindu, Buddhist, or otherwise— have long advocated the practice of being happy with one's position in life no matter how repellent and depressing it feels like on the surface. Lose your house in a flood? Be thankful that this karmic debt has been paid and no longer waits in the future. Leprosy? Better now than later. Few cultures can compete with India's when it comes to accepting life as it is rather than just as one would like it to be.

To Do or Not to Do

Registration day arrived, and with nothing decided upon, I wandered blankly through a vast lecture hall full of tables, each with the name and number of a class taped to the front of it, and a line of purposeful-looking students waiting their turn to sign up. One of these tables was labeled "Beginning Chinese." There was no line of students, so I wrote my name on the list. At the very least, I reasoned, a knowledge of the Chinese language would leave me better equipped to study the *Tao-te Ching* without the distortions of Western translators.

With one actual class under my belt, I began to peruse the other desks more confidently, and before long had added my name to four other lists: Music 105, Art History 105, Beginning Sculpture, and something called World Religions.

Sleeping and Waking

Freedom of activity is never achieved by abstaining from action. Nobody can become perfect by merely ceasing to act. In fact, nobody can ever rest from his activity even for a moment. . . . The world is imprisoned in its own activity. . . . Therefore you must perform every action sacramentally, and be free from all attachment to results.

—BHAGAVAD GITA

Even before the Age of Science came along to tell everyone that the universe was one big machine full of little machines competing with each other for fuel, one of the great threats to the individual with a view to becoming an Adult Unlike Other

Adults was automatism. Actual machines didn't need to exist for the world's wisdom traditions to understand that human beings are susceptible to "mechanical" states of mind, and that unless they are careful, they risk going through their entire lives as sleepwalkers.

In *Zen and the Art of Motorcycle Maintenance*, Robert Pirsig begins the account of his machine-powered journey in search of truth with a description of the difference between major highways and the smaller roads that he prefers to travel on. "On Labor Day and Memorial Day weekends we travel for miles on these roads without seeing another vehicle, then cross a federal highway and look at cars strung bumper to bumper to the horizon. Scowling faces inside. Kids crying in the back seat. I keep wishing there were some way to tell them something but they scowl and appear to be in a hurry, and there isn't. . . ."

Most adults, says Pirsig, echoing Thoreau, who said something quite similar a century or so before, spend their time in "a kind of endless day-to-day shallowness, a monotony that leaves a person wondering years later where all the time went and sorry that it's all gone." In other words, most people are asleep.

That's where the wisdom traditions, and the Adult Unlike Other Adults at their center, come along. By taking a sharp turn off that big gray federal highway called ordinary adulthood, we enter the twisting, turning, challenging, but also deeply gratifying world of the road not taken by most—the alternative route through life described by so many wisdom manuals. Sometimes the details of the metaphor get reversed, and (as in both the Upanishads and the Gospels, among other places) it is the rambling maze of ordinary life that we turn off of, onto the razor-straight track of the way of wisdom. But whichever way it is illustrated, the same basic event is being described.

Whether it is seen as being twisty and turny or relentlessly straight and narrow, the alternate route through life taken by the Adult Unlike Other Adults requires one very important thing of us: that we stay awake—wide-awake—while on it. The ordinary route through life is one that any sleepwalker or robot can stay on. Indeed, sleepwalking robots do better on it than those rare individuals with a genuine awareness of life's shortcomings. But getting onto the alternate route—and staying on it—requires that we have our wits about us at all times.

Conflicting Instructions

And yet, for all that the world's wisdom sources tell us to snap out of it, to open our eyes and see what's really going on in our lives and the urgency of changing those lives into something different than what they are, these same sources also seem to tell us, almost in the same breath, to accept our position in life wholeheartedly, along with all its irritating shortcomings.

Which piece of advice is the one we're really supposed to take?

Probably no book in all of the world's wisdom literature has done a more energetic and successful job of tackling this contradiction than the Bhagavad Gita. Written sometime before the second century B.C., this dialogue between the reluctant warrior Arjuna and his divine chariot-driver Krishna is traditionally tucked away as a chapter within the voluminous *Mahabarata*, one of India's two great national epics. The Bhagavad Gita probably began its life as a separate work, however, and continues to be read outside of the context of the very long and very complicated tale of Indian gods and heroes it officially belongs to.

For centuries, the Bhagavad Gita has been India's single most popular and influential Life Manual, summing up in its

few pages the entire Indian response to life and its conundrums. It was also one of the first exotic wisdom books to be
translated into English in the nineteenth century, when Far
Eastern religious works began coming to the attention of early
American wisdom hunters like Thoreau—who studied a copy
during his days at Walden Pond—and Emerson. Today about a
thousand translations, in thirty or so languages, exist.

Krishna's Answer

To be stuck in the ordinary world, the Gita tells us—as do most
traditional Life Manuals—is to be in trouble. Even at its best,
human life is a honey pot that is equal parts pleasurable sweet-
ness and unpleasant stickiness. To live is inevitably to get
caught up with people and situations that we would much
rather avoid, to do things we don't want to do, to become
things we had never intended to become. Even for people
intent on moving through life with as few entanglements as
possible, simply being alive has a way of making them dirty.
And the more we get involved in all this dirt, the more difficult
it becomes to wash it off ourselves. It becomes all but impossible to pull off of Pirsig's bumper-to-bumper superhighway. Fear
of this, desire of that, habitual attachment to something else—
all of these things come to control people more and more as
time goes by.

And so the great question arises: What do we do when, as
sometimes happens, we wake up a little bit to the reality of this
situation, and see what a mess we are in? Having realized, even
if just for a moment, that at its very best life is still a kind of
trap, how do we react to this news? Do we just stay where we
are, continuing to give in to all of our appetites and petty nagging fears and making do with all the watery little rewards that

life doles out? Or do we slam on the brakes, fold our arms, and refuse to go another inch?

The Bhagavad Gita's famous response to this question is that we should do both . . . and neither. We need to say not yes nor no to life, but yes and no at the same time. If we do so, the Gita tells us, we will come to realize that life is both the place we need to escape from *and* the place we need to be—that it is both a realm of tragedy and tedium, *and* the place where everything works out just as it's supposed to.

The protracted two-person discussion that makes up the bulk of the Bhagavad Gita takes place on the Plain of Kurukshetra, just as a massive battle between rival branches of a warrior family is about to commence. Arjuna, the question-asker in the dialogue, is one of the sons of the deceased King Pandu, a group who together are known as the Pandavas. Pandu also has a nephew named Duryodhana, the villain of the epic, who spends his time making life as difficult for the Pandavas as possible. For a long time the Pandavas put up with Duryodhana's schemes and insults as best they can, but eventually the offenses on Duryodhana's part pile up to a point where war becomes inevitable. The Pandavas range themselves against Duryodhana and his relatives, and all are poised to plunge into battle.

It is at this moment that Arjuna seizes up. Looking out at the field of combat and seeing his friends and relatives preparing for imminent dismemberment and death, he is overcome with doubt. Is the battle, he starts to wonder, really necessary? As a warrior and member of the wronged Pandavas it is his duty to participate, yet suddenly the whole idea nauseates him. What a big, painful, ridiculous waste of time the whole thing is.

Krishna, Arjuna's companion in the chariot, is really Brahman—God himself—in disguise and has incarnated as Arjuna's chariot-driver for the purpose of explaining life to him (a fact that Arjuna seems at one moment to be aware of and at others to forget). At this crucial moment of indecision, Arjuna turns to Krishna and poses the question that the Bhagavad Gita will spend much of the rest of its length answering. "Which," Arjuna asks, "will be worse, to win this war, or to lose it? I scarcely know." It is the same question, of course, that most people at some point or other end up asking about their own lives.

Learned Foolery

A day or so after registration, I found myself in the campus bookstore, examining the texts that I would be reading in my upcoming classes. I was not particularly excited about this project, as I knew that textbooks could always be counted on to be dull no matter what topic they were discussing. This was to be expected because textbooks were written by academics, and academics, as a breed, tended to miss the point of what life was really all about. As Huxley had declared in *The Doors of Perception*, "there is always money for, there are always doctorates in, the learned foolery of research into what, for scholars, is the all-important problem: Who influenced whom to say what and when? Even in this age of technology the verbal Humanities are honored. The non-verbal humanities, the arts of being directly aware of the given facts of our existence, are almost completely ignored."

Clearly things had not changed much in the twenty-plus years since Huxley had penned these lines. My textbook for Beginning Chinese, once I located it among the shelves, lay heavy in my hands like a phone directory for the city of the dead. Opening it at random, I was confronted with column upon column of alien squiggles—squiggles that for some reason lacked the romantic look of the Chinese characters that occasionally decorated the margins of my Chinese wisdom books. It was hard to imagine ever being on friendly terms with such a book. But of course, language texts always looked dull. Perhaps over in World Religions things would pep up a bit.

Such proved not to be the case, however. In fact, that shelf held even bleaker news. The course had six principal texts, all published by the same company, which lay stacked up like ammunition for some great war against all that was vital and interesting in life. Islam. Hinduism. Buddhism. Chinese Religions. Judaism. Christianity. Each had a fearfully dull-looking volume dedicated to it. Could someone really be expecting me to read these? Beaten and dispirited, I wandered over into the section of the store where the noncourse books were on sale. I found Eastern Religion and began browsing.

Almost immediately, a title jumped out at me. The *Bhagavad Gita*, or *Song of God*, with an introduction by Aldous Huxley. I picked it up and flipped to the end. A hundred and forty-three pages: a little long, but promising all the same. Leaving my course texts for another day, I bought it and headed back to my room.

Krishna to the Rescue

Classes commenced the following week, and I found myself dragging right out of the starting gate. World Religions got the ball rolling with Judaism, a religion whose dangerous dualistic tendencies and legalistic, patriarchal preoccupations I had already been thoroughly warned about by writers like Watts and Huxley. For all its prestige as a Life Manual for countless generations, the Bible—and particularly the Book of Genesis—was simply too thorny and weird a piece of literature for me to be able to linger with for long, especially given the failing marks just about all of my Life Manuals gave it. The first family of Genesis were an awfully peculiar bunch to be emulating, as far as I could see. Why all the fuss and discussion about these people who, when not wailing at God for not having given them enough land or children, were constantly killing, raping, or double-crossing each other? *Tanakh. Shofet. Ketuvim. Mishnah. Halakhah. Haggadah. Sedarim. Nezikim. Teharot.* What was a disaffected, Way-walking WASP like me to do with all these alien names, customs, and concepts? Probably there was stuff of value to be learned somewhere within this jungle of consonants, just as there also might be within what seemed the scarcely less puzzling, cluttered, and bureaucratic cosmos of Christianity. (I was well aware, for instance, that Jesus, when not going on tediously about being the only-begotten son of God and all that, had come up with a good number of appealing pronouncements about simplicity, humility, and other such Tao-flavored subjects.) But I didn't have time to go digging for the stray wise morsels hidden here and there in that great stew of Judeo-Christian complexity. There was better hunting to be had elsewhere.

Beginning Chinese was almost equally problematic. The simplest sentences took endless repetition to master, and such English as was spoken in class was entirely too full of talk about economics, job possibilities in the United Nations, and other such nonmystical fare. After some eight years of this, I could apparently hope to read a Beijing newspaper with some facility. Though I knew the men of the ancient Way had possessed the patience of tree stumps and the docility of jellyfish, and that eight years was a blink of an eye when it came to understanding the workings of the Tao, there was a utilitarian flavor to the whole business that just put me off. Even if it meant that, a year or so after mastering that newspaper, I might be able read the *Tao-te Ching* for myself, the effort didn't really seem worth it.

Better, I began to suspect, to walk the unwalkable Way without benefit of a knowledge of Chinese, just as, oddly enough, a couple of the *Tao-te Ching*'s recent "translators" in my library themselves had.

Before long I was bypassing most of my classes and spending my time either wandering aimlessly around campus or sitting in my room reading about Krishna and Arjuna, and the latter's trepidation at getting involved in the ugly business of life—a trepidation that I now identified with 100 percent.

Atman and Brahman

The edition of the Bhagavad Gita that I had stumbled upon in the campus bookstore was the result of a collaboration between Christopher Isherwood and Swami Prabhavananda, one of the first native teachers of Indian mystical philosophy to get established in the United States, and in many ways the archetype for all the countless West Coast guru imports to follow. Throughout the middle decades of the twentieth century, Prabhavananda was the resident Master at the Vedanta Society of southern California—a small, white, exotic-looking building that served as the West Coast nerve center for Eastern wisdom in the years when Huxley, Isherwood, and their fellow British expatriate Gerald Heard were its chief exponents.

Vedanta is perhaps the most vigorous and intellectually developed school of thought in all of Hinduism. Vedanta's focus—central to Hinduism as a whole but attacked there with unique intensity—is the absolute identity of the individual self, or Atman, and the supreme Self: God, or Brahman. With Swami Prabhavananda's help, Isherwood set himself to translating and commenting on the Indian classics that best gave expression to this nondualist philosophy. An edition of the *Yoga Sutras* of Patañjali—a renowned early systematizer of the vast and tangled cosmos of Indian philosophy—came out in 1953 with the boldly unambiguous title *How to Know God*. Along with the Bhagavad Gita, published in 1944, it became a Life Manual classic when it was rereleased as a mass-market paperback in the sixties.

Isherwood and Prabhavananda's works were the place where many a philosophically disaffected American first met and wrestled with such terms as karma, dharma, Brahman, Atman, and nirvana. Such readers learned that Brahman, or God, alone was real, that life in the phenomenal world was maya, or illusion, and that in order for the self, or Atman, to realize its essential oneness with Brahman, it was necessary first to wake up from the sleep of ordinary existence. All actions, Isherwood and his teacher explained, from the good to the bad to the indifferent, participate in maya and hence are uniformly illusory. Brahman alone is ultimately real, and it is the sole essential responsibility of each incarnate being to realize this fact for him- or herself as swiftly and decisively as possible.

Time to pull off the highway.

Pleasure and Pain, Gain and Loss

Or rather, as the Bhagavad Gita explains, time to pull off the highway *without* pulling off, by realizing that all actions are equally grounded in maya on the surface and equally dependent on Brahman at their core. Being stuck on the road of ordinary life isn't a problem as long as you remember what is really going on and perform all actions with a uniform disinterest. As everything is connected to everything else, you can't budge an inch in life without it having consequences of some sort. A person can no more climb out of the vast web of endless cause and effect that makes up incarnate existence than they can climb out of their own skin. The trick, Krishna explains to Arjuna, is to act without acting—to go through life with a mysterious lack of concern for the results of any of the stuff one does—though doing one's best, of course, to do good stuff and not bad. As Isherwood put it in his introduction, "[W]hen action is done in this spirit . . . it will lead us to the knowledge of what is behind action, behind all life: the ultimate Reality."

Nor, Isherwood also promised, did acting in this way make you boring. Surprisingly, this disinterested style of going through life was supposed to produce just the opposite result, making a person lively, vibrant, and as interested in all that went on around him as he himself was interesting to others. In some respects, identifying with Brahman was like taking on the point of view of the camera in a motion picture. Suddenly, marvelously, one found oneself above the action, watching it all from a fluid, all-seeing, and tranquil remove, even while remaining right down there in the very heart of it all. And just as a person could be bored to death with the city or town where he lived yet become oddly fascinated with its every detail if it happened to be featured in a movie, so apparently did all of life slide into a sharp and fascinating focus once the identification with Brahman was achieved. People who did what they did "without thought of the result," as the Bhagavad Gita put it, had a much better time in life than all those worried, unsatisfied sleepwalkers who did stuff only to get benefit from it. Arjuna, Isherwood said in his commentary, was sometimes known as "the conqueror of sloth" because he was "traditionally supposed to have lived entirely without sleep." In other words, he became the ideal example of someone who tooled down the alternate road of life with his eyes wide open, knowing just what the real deal with incarnate existence was, and hence untouched on a deep level by anything that he did or that was done to him. He did what he needed to do—even down to cutting people up with his sword, apparently—but because he was *awake*, all his actions brought him closer to Brahman instead of pushing him further away.

If a person actually managed to learn how to act in this mysterious way, nothing they did and nothing that happened to them could produce any wrong. "Die," says Krishna to the depressed and indecisive Arjuna, "and you win heaven. Conquer, and you enjoy the earth. Stand up now, son of Kunti, and resolve to fight. Realize that pleasure and pain, gain and loss, victory and defeat, are all one and the same: then go into battle. Do this and you cannot commit any sin."

Trees and Fish

Much as I still admired Lao-tzu, the Bhagavad Gita thus taught me that I did not need to actually follow in his footsteps and ride off on a water buffalo to become enlightened. Instead, I could act like Arjuna did following his tutorial session with Krishna: I could march boldly right through the muddy center of life, without any thought of how dirty I got in the process.

But . . . did this mean I had to suffer through World Religions and Beginning Chinese while I did so? Did caring-yet-not-caring about the muddy maya of existence mean I had to memorize the names of all those Jewish rituals and study all those endless Chinese characters? Perhaps the business of putting up with life in a state of magical equanimity could better be accomplished if I was off doing something simpler, rougher, and more elemental: chopping wood in the forests of the Pacific Northwest, for example, or working on a fishing boat far out at sea. A good number of my Life Manual masters had worked at such ordinary-yet-romantic-sounding jobs at some point or other, and the experience always did them a world of good. There was, of course, the catch that I was not on personal terms with any actual lumber cutters or deep-sea fishermen, but I supposed I could track some down if I really put my mind to it.

As more weeks went by, I began to learn the Tao of being a wide-awake but uncommitted, active-yet-inactive college student. I got out of bed every day and did stuff, yet somehow without ever actually doing anything. Meals were eaten, and I attended just enough classes that I was not a complete nonentity to my various professors. Dutifully, I wandered from building to building like all the other students did, with their armfuls of textbooks and their binders with hideously conventional-sounding abbreviations, like Poli-Sci, Econ, and Bio-Chem, lettered boldly across them.

I also discovered how to make peace with the language lab—a subterranean structure in which I was expected to spend a certain number of hours each week listening to a tape cassette repeat phrases like "How are you," "Have you seen my ball-point pen," and "These noodles are delicious" in Chinese. The overheavy headphones at each cubicle made it possible to listen to whatever sort of cassette one wanted, and before long I replaced the tiresome Chinese sentences with tapes from my own collection. Listening to the Rolling Stones, Elvis Costello, or Blondie, I would stare dreamily down at the Chinese characters in my textbook, biding my time.

Off to Battle

Christmas approached, and I realized that, pleasant enough as this new style of school attendance was, it probably wasn't what Krishna had meant when he had given his pep talk to Arjuna. Nor, I imagined, was it what my father had had in mind when he forked over several thousand dollars to the college. So one day I wandered over to the administrative building and declared that I would be taking a season off. It was time to go fire watch in Yosemite, or haul fishnets on the Newfoundland banks, or take on some other rough-and-tumble chore. I was going to cut myself a good thick slice of ordinary life—one that didn't require any rote memorization—and live it with a disinterested vengeance.

For all the campus-organized events designed to force new students to meet and get to know each other, I still had few friends at school. The majority of students seemed to know something I didn't, and the few who looked lost and dazed like I did were no more anxious to talk to me than I was to talk to them. Despite this, I eventually made a few friends in my dorm, and one of these, a girl who had a collection of Life Manuals of her own, offered to read her *I Ching* for me to help me make better sense of my next step in life.

Life Manual classic though it was, the *I Ching* had not managed to intrigue me much thus far. For all its potential Far Eastern allure, it had a crucial number of shortcomings. First of all, it was way too thick. Should one really trust a book with that many pages? I doubted it. I also gathered that it was essentially a Confucian text, and Confucius, most of my Life Manual masters agreed, was something of a fuddy-duddy, his chief use being as a straight man for Taoists to poke fun at. The book also seemed to contain an excessive amount of legalistic mumbo jumbo derived from the political institutions of the day, and that was the last thing I, as a follower of the great Tao, wanted anything to do with.

In spite of my doubts about the text, I eventually let my friend throw her coins for me. The results were less than encouraging.

12. P'i / Standstill [Stagnation]

Heaven and earth are out of communion and all things are benumbed. What is above has no relation to what is below, and on earth confusion and disorder prevail. The dark power is within, the light power is without. Weakness is within, harshness without. Within are the inferior, and without are the superior. The way of inferior people is in ascent; the way of superior people is on the decline.

As my friend read on, I did not find my affection for the *I Ching* increasing. Did this mean I should give up on the idea of leaving school? I suspected not. There were always the book's suspicious Confucian affiliations to keep in mind. Surely Lao-tzu himself would take a dim view of trusting such a volume over what was in one's own heart.

So, with the arrival of Christmas, I left school to seek the Way outside the crumbling walls of the Western paradigm. I gave the steering wheel a good sharp turn, and left Art History 105, Music 105, Beginning Chinese, and World Religions to those better equipped to stomach them. And if the *I Ching* was right about the poor timing of my adventure, that was fine too. After all, as Lao-tzu and the Bhagavad Gita had both now assured me, even when you thought you were stepping outside the bounds of the great Way, you were still well within them, because really going against the Way was impossible. In the last analysis, you were always exactly where you needed to be.

THE MYSTERY OF RELATIONSHIP

Life Is About Relationship

He knows peace who has forgotten desire.

—BHAGAVAD GITA

Stop any New Physicist in the street, and he will explain to you that the entire universe is built upon relationship. Down in the subatomic world nothing "exists" independently, but only comes into being through relating to something else. Move up from quarks and neutrons into the interpersonal domain, and this continues to be the case. Without relationship, it would be impossible for a person to feel that he or she exists, for to exist is by nature to exist in relation *to* something: to other people, to the world and the experience it throws at us, and, not least of all, to that great Something Else that goes by such names as the Tao, the Nagual, Brahman, the Void, the Buddha-nature, or God—depending on the Life Manual in question. To live means to be in relationship, and to live correctly means to master the mystery of relationship and live a life of healthy, vital, meaningful ones rather than sick, misled, destructive ones.

Not that this is necessarily an easy thing to do, for at least in some respects, the question of "right relationship," as the Buddhists call it, is the messiest one of all. In fact, it's so messy that it can't be completely covered in one chapter, but bleeds over into all the others.

In the interpersonal domain, two of the relationships most frequently discussed by Life Manuals are the teacher-student and the romantic varieties. Obviously the former is essential to the Life Manual universe, for without it there could be no interaction between the wisdom neophyte and the Adult Unlike Other Adults who shows him or her the ropes. But how about the latter? Is romance an aid to the getting of wisdom, an impediment, or neither?

The Difference Between Girls and Dogs

If my brief stint at Vassar accomplished little in the way of formal education, it *did* add one element to my life that up to then had been decidedly lacking: a girlfriend. The details of how Elena and I ended up meeting aren't important (and, this being a Life Manual rather than a poignant coming-of-age memoir, I'd just as soon spare her the embarrassment of my recounting them). The pertinent details for our purposes are that she attended the University of Pennsylvania, where I would visit her on weekends, and that she was thoroughly, hopelessly more practical-minded than I could ever dream of being. It only took me a very short time with Elena to learn that the whole how-to-be-an-adult problem I had been wrestling with elsewhere in my life was to plague my dealings in the interpersonal/romantic domain as well.

Elena enjoyed reading books just like I did, but unlike me the books she read were not exclusively Life Manuals. While I had decided on Vassar largely because the trees there were pretty, she had chosen the University of Pennsylvania for a whole plateful of more sensible reasons. She even seemed to know what she wanted to study while there. If my ambivalence toward just about everything in my life other than my little library of wisdom books was at times interesting or charming to Elena—just as her odd practical-mindedness sometimes was to me—it soon became apparent that more often my mystically tinged muddleheadedness simply annoyed her. It turned out that when talking to one's girlfriend one was expected to display a certain range of emotional expression, and that, at least in part because of my Life Manual–engendered suspicion toward the world and all things in it, my emotional range hovered somewhere between zero and one.

Later in life, I would learn that my failings here were not at all unique to me. You didn't have to be lost in a parallel universe of wisdom manuals to be interpersonally challenged, and millions of other young and not-so-young men out there with no mystical leanings whatsoever were idiots in this domain as well. But on those weekends that Elena and I began to spend together toward the tail end of my time at college, it seemed like the malady might be original to me.

My whole relationship with Elena can be encapsulated by an exchange that took place early on in our time together, when I had reached out and given her a spontaneous, friendly pat on the head.

"What are you *doing?*"

"I don't know." (A typical response.)

"I'm not a *dog.* I'm a *girl.* You have to treat girls differently than dogs."

Elena had a point, of course: girls clearly *were* different from dogs. But while this difference was an altogether fine thing in some respects, in others it seemed a bit of a shame. Dogs were pleasant, predictable, *understandable*. Girls, I was quickly learning, were quite often not.

Just because I was as lousy at romance as I was at so many other aspects of adult living didn't mean, however, that the whole topic wasn't of concern to me. For romance was part of relationship, and I understood—in my limited and clumsy way—that relationship was at the root of everything it means to be human in the world. And I knew this for the same reason I knew most of the other important things that I did: my Life Manuals had told me so. Still, the thing about being in an *interpersonal* relationship was that it was so much more problematic than the more rarefied kinds I liked to read about in my wisdom books. Clearly, the issue was a thorny one even for those spiritual athletes who in days past had really lived in accord with the Tao, and Brahman, and all those other wonderfully abstract subjects I felt so at home with. One couldn't help but notice that the greatest masters of those domains all seemed to have been bachelors.

Wisdom Is a Woman

Strangely enough, the group of wisdom authors who arguably have the most to say on the problem of interpersonal relationship hail not from the Far East, as most of my wisdom voices so far did, but from the West—the same West that I was struggling so hard not to learn anything about in my college courses. Wisdom and interpersonal relationship are completely inseparable in the West, and this is because Western wisdom itself, for all its dualistic, mechanistic faults, initially arose out of one very particular and special such relationship: that between many of the West's most important philosophers, and a woman named Sophia.

Sophia, of course, is Greek for wisdom, and she makes her first major appearance in the West as Hokhmah (the Hebrew equivalent of the same word) in Proverbs, where she is described dancing before God at the creation of the world.

"When he established the heavens," says Sophia/Hokhmah, "I was there, when he drew a circle on the face of the deep, when he made firm the skies above, when he established the fountains of the deep, when he assigned to the sea its limit, so that the waters might not transgress his command, when he marked out the foundations of the earth, then I was beside him, like a master workman; and I was daily his delight, rejoicing before him always, rejoicing in his inhabited world and delighting in the sons of men."

Reading this text today, one might be tempted to think that Wisdom is assuming a subordinate place, providing a spectacle for God's enjoyment. Yet it is most likely that Sophia's role at the dawn of Western culture was actually not subordinate but collaborative. In those days the divine creative forces that gave birth to the world could often be seen as feminine—either exclusively or in combination with a masculine force (the Greek Logos, for example), which sometimes existed above the feminine but at others was cradled entirely within it (like the infant Jesus cradled in the arms of his virgin mother).

In the Apocryphal Book of Ben Sirach it is written of Sophia that

> The first man knew her not perfectly: no more shall the last find her out. For her thoughts are more than the sea, and her counsels profounder than the great deep.

Why is wisdom so often personified as female in the West? The answer lies somewhere at the very beginnings of Western thought—in places like Egypt, Babylon, Sumer, Minoan Crete—and perhaps even earlier, with the goddess-oriented cultures of the Neolithic period. "I am all that is and that was and that shall be," proclaims an inscription on an Egyptian temple to the goddess Neith at Saïs, "and no mortal hath lifted my veil." The tradition continues with Plato, for whom, in the *Symposium*, Sophia speaks through the priestess Diotima of the beauty that draws mortals upward from the dross of worldly life to the pristine and super-real dimension of the Platonic Forms. For Plato, wisdom implied the ability to discern the archetypal forces at work amid the apparent confusion and opacity of the merely material, and in the *Symposium* it is Diotima who provides the central impetus for doing so. Here again, the image is of a supremely attractive yet supremely mysterious figure—a feminine embodiment, in some respects, of Emperor Hun Tun—who for all that she attracts us, and for all her tremendous, world-annihilating reality, vanishes in a moment if we approach too swiftly, or in the wrong way. In the Islamic world as well, a long and dazzlingly intricate tradition of mystical writing and verse (exemplified by writers like the thirteenth-century Persian poet Rūmī) centered around similar situations in which a lover encounters a beloved (usually though not always female) who is not simply an earthly object of affection but a doorway into direct experience of the Divine.

The emphasis in these mythic-religious images is again and again on a moment of vision—a moment in which a thinker (typically though not always male) gazes upon a female (either divine or human or, in the case of Dante's Beatrice, seemingly a combination of the two), and in that moment recognizes the limited nature of all that he has experienced in life up to that point. The convergence of feelings this experience creates—love, awe, and the sensation of a fathomless mystery, attractive and potentially consuming—brings about a sort of rebirth. Once he has caught a glimpse of Sophia and the world she opens onto, it becomes the central responsibility and challenge of the true philosopher—

the lover of wisdom—to see the disappointments, and even the outright tragedies, of ordinary life in their proper perspective.

Above and Below

I am well acquainted with the many deceptions of that monster, fortune. She pretends to be friendly to those she intends to cheat, and disappoints those she unexpectedly leaves with intolerable sorrow. If you will recall her nature and habits, you will be convinced that you had nothing much of value when she was with you and you have not lost anything now that she is gone.

—SOPHIA, IN *THE CONSOLATION OF PHILOSOPHY*

Human affairs ought not to be taken very seriously.

—PLATO

One of the Western philosophical tradition's most vivid examples of this transforming confrontation with Sophia appears in Boethius's *The Consolation of Philosophy*, the quintessential Life Manual of medieval Christendom. A prominent Roman statesman in the last days of the Empire, Boethius was also an accomplished scholar. The story goes that often he had taken political office—largely out of a sense of duty rather than desire for the task—Boethius's strong morals and excessive honesty secured him a long list of enemies. Ultimately, some of these succeeded in collecting enough evidence against him— much or all of it specious—to secure his imprisonment, and eventually his execution.

While in his cell awaiting imminent torture and death, Boethius pondered the injustice of life and his wretched misfortune. What sort of a world is it in which, doing what one knows in one's heart is the right thing, one ends up in such miserable straits? In the midst of these thoughts, Boethius writes in the *Consolation* that he was surprised by a vision. "There appeared standing above me a woman of majestic countenance whose flashing eyes seemed wise beyond the ordinary wisdom of men. Her color was bright, suggesting boundless vigor, and yet she seemed so old that she could not be thought of as belonging to our age. Her height seemed to vary: sometimes she seemed of ordinary human stature, then again her head seemed to touch the top of the heavens. And when she raised herself to her full height she penetrated heaven itself, beyond the vision of human eyes."

This is Lady Philosophy—also known as Sophia, also known as Wisdom personified—the same timeless presence who rejoiced before God at the creation of the world, and who through the priestess Diotima led Plato to an understanding of the Forms that live above and beyond the confusion and darkness of mundane experience (and thanks at least in part to whom Plato's own master Socrates had been able to face execution with complete equanimity). When Boethius complains to Sophia of his wretched state and the seeming impossibility of having faith in a world where things so often shake out unfairly for the genuinely honest and just, she explains that he is making a great mistake in giving any lasting weight at all to his present condition. Yes, from an earthly perspective he is indeed in a bad way. Yes, down on the plain of earth the bad frequently attain power by betraying the good. But in the long run all this is really beside the point. For all that evil so often seems to win and virtue to get trodden into the dirt, from the perspective of the larger dimension that the majority of mortals are so blind to, love and goodness always triumph.

Like many a classic Life Manual, the *Consolation* is not original in terms of its material (the ideas in it that can't be traced to Plato can be found in Saint Augustine and the New Testament). Its strength lies rather in its powerful and passionate synthesis of the best thinking of the Greek and Christian past—a synthesis that was to play a large part in keeping that thinking alive throughout the Middle Ages. At the heart of Boethius's synthesis is a firm belief in the centrality of love, and an equation of true wisdom with a living understanding of love's reality. This basic equation of wisdom with love was to remain at the heart of the Western philosophical tradition for centuries—sometimes in plain sight, at other times all but completely hidden. Even with the advent of Newton, Descartes, and all the rest of that great army of mechanistic killjoys, it was never really to be completely eradicated.

Love Versus Loving-Kindness

Not that I knew anything about Boethius during my days at Vassar, or about Dante, or Plato, or Augustine, or any other proponent of the divinely interpersonal component hiding at the heart of the Western wisdom traditions, for that matter. But I did have some knowledge of the novel notion that the solution to the individual's and the world's problems lay in love. After all, every wisdom tradition suggests that this is so at some point—the difference being in how love is defined in each case. For Buddhism and Taoism, for example, the love that saves the world is of a decidedly impersonal nature, and is better named by a term like compassion or loving-kindness. The chief difference with the wisdom traditions of the West is that when they offer up love as the one true answer to all life's questions, they tend to do it personally—so personally, in fact, that in Christianity, Judaism, and Islam, that love revolves around the notion of a God who is himself a Person.

Being on the run from the Western tradition, and using for my wisdom sources a group of books written primarily by modern Western men who were in all-out flight from that heritage as well, my tools for figuring out whether romantic love was a bust or not were of course primarily Eastern. And the answer they tended to give was that yes, it was a bust indeed. Remarkably often in these Eastern-oriented books, the whole deeply charged and polyvalent mystery known as romantic love was simply picked up and dropped into a beaker labeled "attachment." And along with it went Romeo and Juliet, Tristan and Isolde, Dante and the Troubadours, and all the long parade of other Western figures, both real and imagined, who had found in personal love a model upon which to build the very foundations of wisdom.

Reading the materials that I had deemed acceptable for my quest, I thus had little choice but to become even more suspicious of love as a road to happiness than I already might have been. Like adulthood itself, love came with warning labels all over it, and if I was not prepared to take those labels so seriously as not to have a girlfriend at all, I *was* ready to take them seriously enough to ensure that I made her miserable most of the time. Not only had Elena found one of the countless young males out there who wasn't up to mastering the complexities of an interpersonal relationship—she had also found one who was coming to see this inability as a kind of duty.

The Path of Lust

The closest my Life Manuals of the moment came to telling me something really positive about the world of interpersonal relationship was, strangely enough, in the domain of sex. Here again, though, the conclusions to be drawn were only mixed at best.

According to the majority of my Life Manuals (and I certainly had no problem believing them on this), human beings spent most of their time hopelessly in the grip of sexual attraction. One either ground through life meditating constantly on gratifications that one wasn't having, prey to endless erotic fantasies that crowded the imagination like passengers on a stalled subway car in midsummer, or else one was of a more active bent, not suffering these fantasies passively but seeking the sexual partners necessary to fulfill them. If the former sounded like pretty grim going, the latter wasn't much of a winning proposition either, for the one thing that sexual gratification guaranteed was the need in the future—the very near future—for more of it. And more of it, and more of it, and so on, until one was old and broken down and unable to fulfill those desires at all. And even then, my Life Manuals assured me, the desire for further gratifications, and all the hideous karmic entanglements that went along with them, didn't go away, but plagued over-the-hill pleasure seekers with the same merciless gusto they had in younger days.

For all the grimness of this picture, one could, according to some of my wisdom books, actively engage in the world of sexuality and end up further along down the path of wisdom for having done so. Sexuality was still a problem, sure—but only until one had succeeded in understanding and harnessing its powers in the service of getting enlightened.

Watts, with characteristic simplicity and directness, boiled the whole sex-as-path-to-enlightenment project down to a single point: the orgasm. The world, he reminded me once again, is absolutely, ecstatically all right just as it is. The Adult Unlike Other Adults not only knows this but *feels* it, right down to his toes. Most other people, however, being woefully hampered by a vast load of societally imposed preconceptions heaped gradually on them since earliest childhood, are simply incapable of accessing such an attitude of joyous and all-embracing acceptance. For many such people, the sole respite from their closed-off state of mind arrives at the moment of orgasm. During this event, even the most thickheaded materialist could be knocked off the rails and forced to give the universe a big thumbs-up for a second or two. This being the case, the trick was to use the orgasm as a sort of magic rabbit hole, following it down and out of the landscape of unenlightened ordinariness, and into a place where one could be really and truly satisfied with one's existence at all times.

Winning as this strategy sounded, somehow or other it never carried that much weight with me. Watts might have been onto something, but as any bored fourteen-year-old could tell you, the vantage point on the world's essential all-rightness provided by the orgasm was the very definition of fleeting. What were the chances of somehow actually climbing into this psycho-physical state of mind and hammering it into a larger, more lasting perch from which to view the world?

This wasn't the only positive wisdom-approved perspective on sex around. Other authors—and Watts himself in other places in his books—made much of a very different kind of discipline in which the orgasm was not put on a pedestal but instead all but completely removed from the proceedings. Rather than dissipate himself by squandering his precious *chi* energy, or *prana*, or whatever it happened to be called by this book or that, the adept at these practices turned the sexual act into a marathon event that went on for hour upon hour and even day upon day, and which culminated at last not in some mundane spasmodic transfer of bodily fluid but with the actual transformation of both partners into a higher mode of being. The couple who managed it correctly were in fact said by the ancient texts to become semidivine through the process.

They all sounded interesting enough, these strategies for surfing the waves of sexual energy locked up within oneself rather than getting hopelessly jumbled and tumbled by them the way ordinary people so often did. But could the average confused teenager, struggling with the twisting garden hose of sexuality, really make use of such exalted spiritual gymnastics—even provided he or she was able to understand what they were about in the first place? No wonder Lao-tzu hadn't taken anyone along with him on that water buffalo.

C H A P T E R 4

THE ZEN OF WORK

Find Work, Get Enlightened

Between the stages of apprenticeship and mastership there lie
long and eventful years of untiring practice.

—EUGEN HERRIGEL

Once extricated from college, I would find something to do,
and then get enlightened in the process of doing it. A simple
enough plan, but certainly not without its scary aspects. To
begin with, I was still very much up in the air as to what this
enlightenment-inducing, cash-earning labor of mine was to be.
Coming as I did from a family that for generations had been
used to having money around, but which now seemed to have
used most of it up, I had confusingly contradictory views on
the subject built into me. According to my father, worrying
about where the next check was coming from was basically a
waste of one's time. In the end some cash always showed up, so
you might as well just do what you really felt like doing and

hope for the best (or, as the current Life Manual–style cliché puts it, "Do what you love, the money will follow").

Yet in spite of all this apparent disinterest in lowly issues of finance, the subject of cash hovered continually over my parents' household. For something that you weren't supposed to worry about, money showed up in conversations with curious frequency.

One of the main reasons for my family's current mixed-up relationship with money was a book—a book that was almost, but not quite, a Life Manual, and which had been written by none other than my father. After years of bohemian-style struggle on the fringes of his formerly wealthy family, my father had exploded into momentary financial security through his book *The Secret Life of Plants*. When someone spends much of his life doing something that is supposed to be financially irresponsible and at last ends up with money anyhow, the result can be a certain flippancy about the whole subject. Once deposed from its throne, the almighty dollar was chased out of our house with an exuberance bordering on vengefulness.

That had been in the early seventies, and it was now 1981. While all of us in my father's immediate circle were still by and large basking on the upper decks of the money boat, there was no question that it was starting to list distressingly to one side, and warning lights were flickering on from stem to stern. The near future did not look particularly good, financially speaking, but up on the captain's deck my father didn't want to hear anything about it. What—money again? Not on his life was he going to go back to kowtowing to *that* old tyrant.

If my father tended to dismiss all the unmistakable evidence of the uncertain financial future that was now well on its way toward us, my stepmother—who had entered my father's life with her own finances and who was used to managing them along more conventional lines—took a far darker and more realistic view of the situation. Increasingly, she would take me aside and confide to me about the necessity of getting a firmer hand on what I was to do with my life careerwise. Things were not always going to be as plush as they were at the moment, and I would be better off getting used to this fact now rather than later. My sister, too, when we saw each other, did her best to warn me about what actual life, rather than life as my father saw and described it, was probably going to be like for me out there in the world, and what I might best do to prepare for it.

The trouble was that along with these realistic, nuts-and-bolts communiqués, I continued to receive other, entirely contrary ones—from my father mostly, but even from my stepmother when she was in a brighter mood. Again and again, the idea came across that in matters of finance, attitude counted for a great deal, and that if one assumed that things would go badly, they would indeed do so. The possibility persisted that rather than fret about what would happen when the money ran out, I was better off continuing to follow my natural inclinations and thinking positively while doing so. Maybe—just maybe—that would be enough.

However numbered my days of financial security were, it wasn't as if my great aim in life was to be a rich-boy layabout. Wisdom, not languor, was what I was after, and according to my reading of the moment, work was in fact the best way to go about getting it. The Bhagavad Gita made it plain that a person could achieve perfection by devoting himself to "the work which is natural to him." But what work was this? In ancient Indian days, thanks to such amenities as the caste system and an ironclad faith in the laws of karma and rebirth, the question was, once again, a lot easier to answer. Born to merchant parents? Be a merchant! Born to corpse burners on the banks of the Ganges? Burn those corpses then! It was all so straightforward.

Even though my position was obviously more complicated

than this, it was still clear that I shouldn't be too fussy about the job I was after. If the theory of enlightenment-through-work really was a viable one, any old job, from urinal scrubbing to hot dog vending to toll collecting, should do the trick. Back in India it was common knowledge that the most exalted prince and the lowliest untouchable were equally well supplied with opportunities to rediscover their essential unity with Brahman. The real challenge lay in taking advantage of these opportunities instead of just letting them slip by. What I actually did was largely irrelevant.

Still, all things being equal, I might as well find something to do that wasn't *that* unpleasant.

The Closest Thing Around to an Adult Unlike Other Adults

Before I was out of school a month, precisely such a job—one that was neither too fancy nor too menial, neither too bland nor too exciting—came along. My father had for some time owned a very large house in Cartagena, Colombia. I now learned that my photographer stepbrother Nicky was planning a trip there, with the intention of using the house as a base for a series of journeys into the Colombian interior to photograph the countryside and its people. The camera Nicky planned to use for the project was large, old-fashioned, and unwieldy. It took single-loading film cartridges, each one larger than an outstretched hand, which needed to be fed into the camera one at a time. There was in general a lot of folding and unfolding, screwing and unscrewing, and packing and unpacking involved in the camera's use—not to mention the labor of just carrying it around. Nicky would have a tough time doing all of this by himself. Why didn't I accompany him on the trip, working as a sort of camera caddie and general assistant? My father, using some of the last of his mysterious financial reserves, would supply the initial funding, which later might be made back when the pictures were used for some project or other—a book, perhaps.

Nicky was eight years older than I and had been in my life for about a decade, ever since his mother had taken up with my father back in 1970. Close enough to me that I considered him an actual relative, but distanced enough from my day-to-day life to have a slight aura of mystery about him, Nicky had one crucial thing going for him that none of the other adults in my vicinity did. About three years before, he had become a Buddhist. Seemingly out of the blue, he had actually taken that mysterious turn off the highway of ordinary existence that I was now so used to reading about, shocking those around him with a whole new menu of habits and activities entirely out of keeping with his former privileged lifestyle. Used up to then to moving among fancy people in fancy surroundings, Nicky now subjected the details of his life to a radical simplification. He cut out alcohol and all other mind-altering substances from mild to strong. He moved into a crummy New York apartment in a crummy New York neighborhood. He even shaved his head.

I had monitored these changes in Nicky's lifestyle closely, often picking up useful tips from him on ways of conducting myself in my own life. Some months after he had shaved his head, for example, I gave it a try, too, and was delighted with the results. "He must be copying Nicky," I often heard the puzzled adults around me remark in the wake of this experiment— an explanation that, to my mind, missed the point entirely. Sure I was copying him, but only insofar as someone who is lost in a desert "copies" someone else who has found a spring of water and is drinking from it. Having Nicky on the periphery of my life provided me with the nearest thing I had to a role model for the transformed adult I so wished to become. If, simply by virtue of the fact that he existed in three dimensions and I actually knew him, Nicky could not *be* an Adult Unlike Other Adults in my eyes, he was certainly the closest I had gotten to one so far.

Diving into the Dullness

To date, the Life Manual issue that Nicky had managed to get me thinking about most intensely was the problem of time—specifically, the dead spaces that could fill up the day when there wasn't anything in particular to do, or when the things that one did have to do were boring. At the end of the previous summer, just before I entered Vassar, Nicky and I had spent a few weeks together in a cabin on an island off the coast of Maine. The cabin was very small and primitive, dark in the daytime as well as at night, and offered little—or rather nothing—in the way of amusements. It was within this scenic but intensively uneventful atmosphere that I began to fully appreciate the changes that Nicky's new way of thinking were having on his daily life. Lying on my lumpy mattress in the half-light of the cabin's interior, I would read for a while in the morning, then find myself getting bored. Endless and flat, the heart of the day loomed before me—absent of event, devoid of stimulus. The "old" Nicky—the one who went to nightclubs and hung out with famous people—would no doubt have had a similar feeling about these great blocks of empty time. Not, however, the new Nicky. Armed with the structure and purpose of his Buddhist discipline, Nicky managed to navigate these hours with surprising sureness. He fasted. He studied. He tramped off into the woods to meditate, returning covered in bites from mosquitoes that he had refused to slap on the theory that each had been his mother countless times in previous incarnations. He even proclaimed one of our days at the cabin a "no talk day," thus mercilessly removing one of the last crucial time-frittering tools available to me.

After a week or ten days of this, life at the cabin was livened up by the arrival of family friends in a house at the other end of the island. This rescued us—or me—from our daily grind of intensive nonactivity, and I couldn't have been more grateful for it. But after they were over, our "empty" days stuck in my memory. Unlike just about everybody else I knew, Nicky seemed to be preparing for a life in which very, very little happened . . . at least on the surface. More than familiar with all the weapons that the modern world provides for combating the duller moments of life, he seemed intent on plunging straight into those moments and getting something of value out of them. Could he really succeed at such a task, or was he just fooling himself? I was curious to study him further to find out.

Two Brands of Buddhism

Another aspect of Nicky's new lifestyle that fascinated but puzzled me was the particular brand of Buddhism he had chosen for himself. This was Tibetan Buddhism, which in 1980 was not the heavy contender in the Life Manual marketplace that it is today. Books like Sogyal Rinpoche's *Tibetan Book of Living and Dying* were far in the future. The Dalai Lama had yet to become a household name, and no movie or rock stars appeared in magazines waving Tibetan prayer flags or protesting the Chinese invasion of 1959. In fact, Nicky's choice seemed almost willfully obscure to me. This was especially the case as another, entirely more attractive variety of Buddhism was at the time being vigorously and skillfully advertised in a virtual army of Life Manuals. This lighter, breezier, more market-friendly brand of Buddhism was of course Zen. My diet of Zen-flavored Life Manuals had been increasing steadily for some time now, and the more of them I read the more I found to like. Tramping around through the jungles of Colombia carrying Nicky's camera for him might yield interesting clues as to why he had seized upon such a recondite form of Buddhism when this more appealing one lay so close at hand. While getting the hang of the whole work-as-path-to-enlightenment thing that the Bhagavad Gita had got me thinking about, and further studying how Nicky managed the mysterious project of living a boring life without actually being bored, I could also engage in some hands-on comparative wisdom shopping. All in all, it was a perfect solution to my dilemma.

Enlightenment in a Plain Brown Wrapper

If the Bhagavad Gita gives Life Manual literature's most inspired pep talk for saying yes to life in the world and all the assorted chores and obligations that go along with it, Zen literature does the best job of making this task actually sound like fun. A good Zen-flavored Life Manual can make ordinary life, ordinary work, and even ordinary problems seem suddenly, mysteriously interesting. By upsetting our habitual distinctions between what is boring and what is interesting, what is mundane and what is miraculous, Zen writings at their most effective turn the plain, tasteless tap water of regular life into something we actually *want* to drink rather than something we simply have to.

Largely because of its attractiveness to the Beats, Zen was the first exotic spiritual import to completely saturate the American public imagination. It had already done so by the mid-sixties, and by the time I was coming to it in the late seventies, the mischievous, squinty-eyed, paradox-spouting Zen master had achieved the status of a bona fide American cliché. Yet even for all its superficial familiarity, Zen's version of the alternate route through life and the Adult Unlike Other Adults who walks it was so compelling and streamlined that it continued to fire imaginations long after years of overexposure should have cheapened it to death.

The Buddha Wakes Up

Countless writers presenting Zen to modern Western audiences have described how the Buddha, sitting beneath the Bodhi tree in the fifth century B.C., awakened in a single flashing instant to the true nature of human existence and the real solution to all the problems that go along with it. In that blast of insight, we are told, all the tiresome hardware of belief and superstition that had hampered human efforts to make sense of life up until then were rendered null and void. Life, said the Buddha, is suffering. Suffering comes from desire and attachment. And desire and attachment come in their turn from the mistaken notion that anything in life really exists in a deep and lasting manner. In truth, said the Buddha, all is sunyata—a Sanskrit word meaning emptiness or essential insubstantiality. The moment a person awakens to this fact, the Buddha explained, all pain and all problems vanish. Or rather, they don't really vanish so much as it is realized that they never possessed any inherent existence to begin with.

When the Buddha said that everything was characterized by sunyata, he meant everything. For all its endless gods and goddesses and heroes and heroines, for all its epic tales and complicated doctrines, Hinduism was clear in its insistence that Brahman was the only fundamental reality, in relation to which all else was maya, or illusion. Nor had there ever been any question for Hinduism that the human soul's supreme happiness and fulfillment lay in realizing this fact. In his moment of illumination under the Bodhi tree, the Buddha pushed all this a step further by proclaiming that Brahman, too, was an illusion. The self did not suffer, as in Hinduism (and in all the other theistic religions, too, for that matter), because it had forgotten its primordial and irremovable oneness with God. It suffered because it was under the mistaken notion that either self *or* God possessed ultimate existence at all. Not only was there nothing to desire, there was also no one to do the desiring. All was empty.

The Usual Complications

When you are analyzing, you are not looking.

—J. KRISHNAMURTI, *THE AWAKENING OF INTELLIGENCE*

Depending on which Life Manual you listened to, these revolutionary insights of the Buddha's weren't actually all *that* revolutionary, for their outline was visible in the teachings of mystics who had come before him—most particularly the Taoists, whose talk of a pregnant emptiness that gave birth to the manifest world sometimes sounds very much like the Buddha's doctrine of sunyata. But whether or not he was really the first person to have had this experience of a fundamental and all-encompassing emptiness, the Buddha was the one who first described it in a way that could really benefit other people with minimum fuss. In the form in which he first laid it out, the Buddha's program for life and how to live it had about it the terse, pragmatic urgency of the directions on the back of a medicine bottle.

Not that it all stayed as simple as this for very long. People being people, the Buddha's shattering pronouncements on sunyata and its realization were soon being clouded up with a whole new array of gods and goddesses, heavens and hells, and rules and prescriptions as multilayered and confusing as any that had come before. Scarcely had the Buddha uttered the news that all was empty and set forth his bare-bones doctrine for realizing this fact in the depths of one's being, than the doctrine itself started filling up with unnecessary baggage. The lesson of Emperor Hun Tun was being repeated.

It was up to the early masters of Zen—first in Taoist China and later in Japan—to bring the Buddha's message back to the elemental simplicity that it had started with, and to learn how to keep it that way from then on. Zen is in fact a marriage of Buddhist and Taoist ideas: one in which two ways of thinking obsessed with keeping things simple combined to form a way of thinking even simpler and more streamlined than either of its parents. Zen shucked the religious project down to its essence, once and for all tossing those gods and goddesses, heavens and hells, and various arbitrary rules and regulations common to other paths into the trash. If Buddhism is the rotary engine of world religions, then Zen is the rotary engine of Buddhism. It takes the Buddha's clean, no-nonsense pronouncements about the pain of life and its solution and presents them in a style—rigorous yet relaxed, severe yet humorous, sensible yet paradoxical—designed to keep them from getting muddied up with needless complications ever again.

Enlightenment in the Tropics

Nicky's and my first stop in Colombia was my father's house in Cartagena. Three stories high, the place dated from the Colonial era and took up most of one end of a busy, narrow street in the old part of the city. The house had actually been two houses before my father broke down the wall dividing them. Rooms large and small now surrounded a courtyard holding a rich tropical garden open to the sky. From certain of these rooms the nearby sea was visible, and in the afternoons a warm ocean wind flowed over the walls and moved gently through the whole place, opening and slamming doors, rocking the tropical plants in the central garden, and generally relieving the long, merciless heat of midday.

My father had picked up this weird, luxurious, white elephant of a house more or less on a whim back in the heart of his money days, and for some years now it had been functioning largely as a sort of black hole on the edge of his galaxy of influence, steadily sucking the last stray scraps of his cash reserves into itself. I had never spent much time in it before, but now would presumably be staying there on and off for a period of months, in between voyages into the Colombian interior. Nicky had some research to do and permits to obtain in the city before we commenced our initial trip into the bush, so for the moment I had nothing to do but sit around and think some more—much in the way I had been doing ever since leaving high school. Nicky suggested I read some books on Colombia to get a sense of background for our upcoming trips, but I had a stack of Life Manuals to attend to and so ignored this advice.

The house was well suited to contemplative inactivity. Though it sat amid a bustling city, within its walls an atmosphere of singular and intractable stasis prevailed. Just about everybody seemed to slow down a bit when they passed through its doors, and even the laborers my father was employing to finish up on the house's endless construction and renovation projects looked at a loss most of the time, wandering from this room to that carrying a hammer or a half-empty sack of concrete like something they had just come across and didn't quite know what to do with. In the blink of an eye, I had left the world of Econ, Poli-Sci, and Bio-Chem far behind.

Fernando

In spite of the mood of Colonial-style languor that hung over it, there was still plenty going on in the house. Paco and Jodi, the young American couple who looked after it for my father, ran a popular and lucrative restaurant in the new part of the city, and because of their presence a steady stream of people— American and European expatriates and a variety of Colombians as well—came and went at all times. Among the most frequent visitors was a gentleman named Fernando de Uribe. Somewhere in his sixties, Fernando lived next door to us with his wife, Isabella, in a house almost as large and imposing as my father's. A painter of no small repute in Colombia, Fernando spent the day producing large, colorful canvases featuring a recurring retinue of black bulls, big-breasted women, and predatory-looking sea fish. Fernando had long been friends with Paco and Jodi, and when the breezy late afternoon hours arrived and his painting was behind him for the day, he liked to come over and unwind.

Fernando looked, acted, and even smelled the way I figured an artist was supposed to. Short and wiry, with bowlegs and a bristly gray mustache seasoned to brown in places from endless Pielroja cigarettes—the stubby, filterless brand that everyone in Cartagena smoked—he radiated heat and energy like a car engine on a hot summer day. Stalking back and forth in his uniform of sandals, ragged cutoff shorts, and paint-spattered T-shirt, Fernando was quick to get across that he was a man who was just nuts about the world and everything in it. He spoke good English, but would lapse into Spanish when he got especially worked up about something—and when he got really, really excited he would give up on speech entirely. Sinking his strong, tanned, paint-mottled fingers into my shoulders like a bird of prey, he would stare at me for long moments, his face pushed up close to mine, grinning with wordless intensity. Just at the point when this might have started to get uncomfortable, Fernando would sum up his feelings with a single, all-encompassing word.

"*Chévere. Chévere, Ptolomeo! Sí, sí, chévere.*"

Though it was resistant to translation, *chévere* apparently meant something like "good." What exactly was Fernando affirming in these impassioned moments? It was never completely clear, but I got the idea that it was life in general that was getting the big thumbs-up. After all, being an artist, it was Fernando's job to have an extra-enthusiastic attitude about the world and all it held.

It didn't take too long for me to realize that Fernando's constantly energized attitude had something to do with another important Colombian product that, along with Pielroja cigarettes, he went through in great quantity. This was Tres Esquinas, or Three Corners, rum—apparently named for the triangular shape of the bottle it came in. Fernando guzzled the clear, turpentiney stuff like water, and the more of it he drank, the more *chévere* the world around him became. Late in the evenings, Fernando would often climb into his little Renault town car and tool off into the warm Colombian night in search of further adventures. Weaving this comically small and vulnerable machine through Cartagena's narrow, treacherous streets—often with the headlights out—he would somehow always manage to make it home to paint for another day. On one occasion, in the small hours of the morning, Fernando had taken a gun and blown a hole in an enormous self-portrait he had been working on for weeks. "To truly know yourself," he had explained following this event, "it is necessary to kill yourself!" But Fernando wasn't fooling anybody as far as the possibility of killing himself went. He liked life entirely too much for that—and life, somehow, liked him in return. Like a good man of the Tao, he moved with the flow of things, and this attitude seemed to allow him to get away with all sorts of nonsense without getting into the trouble that normal people would.

Positive and Negative

During our first few weeks in Colombia, Fernando became instructive to me as a living demonstration of a Life Manual lesson I had been encountering more and more in my reading. Once off the main road of ordinary life, it turned out that there was a choice between two basic and very different lifestyles facing the aspiring Adult Unlike Other Adults. This choice had to do with that old problem of "attachments."

For a while, I had started to get the idea that becoming an Adult Unlike Other Adults meant saying good-bye to the sort of vices that made life tolerable for so many ordinary adults— before I had even had a chance to really try any of them out. Could a genuine Adult Unlike Other Adults chug through life fueled constantly by things like Pielrojas and Tres Esquinas, as Fernando so obviously did? Initially I didn't think so, but like so much else in the Life Manual world, the issue turned out to be more complicated than I had at first suspected.

For most Life Manuals, smoking, drinking, womanizing, and the rest of life's higher-octane pleasures were looked upon with suspicion at best. Reading the Bhagavad Gita, for example, you didn't get the idea that Krishna wanted Arjuna devoting his actions to all-mighty Brahman with a martini in one hand and a cigarette in the other. Likewise, Buddha himself had been more than clear that chasing after pleasures was exactly what kept most people from the understanding of ultimate emptiness that was their only true salvation. However, in other areas of the Life Manual landscape—most particularly in some of the writings on Zen that I was now exploring—things weren't quite so simple. Certain versions of the Adult Unlike Other Adults, it developed, were allowed a greater ration of treats and enjoyments than others. Typically, these were the artistic types—individuals who not only didn't fit the mold of ordinary life but were quirky from the standpoint of the enlightened minority as well.

These individuals weren't just noisy, egotistic blowhards, mind you. It wasn't like every idiot with a beard and a paint-brush had special dispensation to have all the fun he wanted and still be enlightened. No—these alternative adults were genuinely different from the mass of ordinary people. They had simply returned from the unspeakable regions of Mind at Large, or Brahman, or sunyata, or wherever, without the incli-nation to be done with all the various and sundry sensual pleas-ures that did such a good job of preventing ordinary people from ever reaching enlightenment to begin with. So it was that there were apparently chain-smoking swamis, womanizing gurus, and drunken Zen artists who made wild pictures by sticking their heads in paint pots and slapping their hair across the canvas. These individuals could continue to enjoy pleasures normally forbidden to the earnest seeker of enlightenment because they were immune to the magnetic pull these pleasures exercised on most people. They could have them precisely because they managed not to care about them to the point of attachment; and if some prudish part of me felt like judging such individuals, that just showed I didn't understand what real enlightenment was all about.

Nor did things stop there, either. The issue was more com-plicated still. Not only did some people, having found their way into the much sought-after domains of genuine enlighten-ment, choose to keep on enjoying this or that worldly vice once they returned to ordinary life. Some of my wisdom writ-ers even insisted that vices themselves could, with luck and some talent, actually *help* a person to achieve enlightenment in the first place. The road of excess could, at times at least, lead to the palace of wisdom. The basic idea was that just about anything a person did could help get him or her to enlightenment, and anything could prevent him or her from getting there as well. It was all a matter of attitude. And in any case, it was highly erroneous to think that enlightenment, being completely beyond such dualistic issues as subject and object, self and other, good-for-you and bad-for-you, was simply something that you could get by performing or refusing to perform actions of any sort. How could it be, when in reality there was no "you" to do the getting to begin with?

Enlightenment's the Thing

Pertinent as Fernando clearly was to these knotty issues, it wasn't like I thought he actually *was* one of these rare enlightened beings with special dispensation to do whatever they liked in life. Like Nicky, he was simply too accessible to me to gain official Adult Unlike Other Adults status in my eyes. But this didn't mean he couldn't be of didactic use all the same, just as Nicky was in his different way. In fact, Fernando was just the counterbalance to Nicky I needed at that moment. Together, they quite clearly marked off opposing ends of the spectrum in terms of the attitudes you could strike toward the wisdom-getting process. Somewhere between Nicky, with his admirable if somewhat intimidating ability to go off and meditate all the time without getting bored or depressed, and Fernando, with his contrasting ability to indulge himself and do crazy stuff without apparent consequence, lay an attitude toward the world and all the things in it that would work for me. But I still didn't know how to find my way into that specific attitude.

There was no question in my mind, however, that the Zen

writings I was now exploring, with their single-minded emphasis on achieving the condition of enlightenment, held important clues. Getting enlightened, said my Zen writers, was the
one really important thing in life. You could spend all the time
you wanted trying to think and act the way an Enlightened
One was supposed to think and act, but this was really just the
kind of misunderstanding that the Buddha, and the Zen masters
who came after him, frowned upon so unanimously. Instead,
one should stop imitating and actually *get* enlightened, and
then all the other problems that an aspiring Adult Unlike Other
Adults faced—problems about what to do or what not to do,
what to like and what not to like, what to renounce and what
not to renounce—would eventually take care of themselves.

Into the Jungle

After a few weeks of sitting around puzzling over these issues
amid the weird, ungainly luxury of my father's house, the
morning came when Nicky announced that preparations were
complete and we were ready for our first trip into the Colombian countryside. We boarded a bus out of the city, and I
steeled myself to commence the simple Zen business of camera
caddying.

   During our weeks at the house, Nicky and I had ventured
out on several afternoons to take some shots of the surrounding
city, so I had already gotten some practice at my new job. So
far, I had to admit that I didn't care too much for it. In fact,
trailing behind Nicky as he fussed and fiddled with all those
lenses, tripods, and film containers was downright tedious.
Nicky had been a meticulous sort even before his Buddhist
inclinations had surfaced three years back, and although he
was patient with me as I struggled to keep his precious gear safe
from the ever-present threats of dust and grime and sunlight, it

was clear that I wasn't especially talented in this area. I dropped stuff. I forgot stuff. I locked boxes that were supposed to be unlocked and unlocked boxes that were supposed to be left locked. My Zen writers had impressed upon me with one voice the idea that a person was supposed to do whatever work a person was doing—no matter how mundane or tedious—as if it were the most important task in the world. It was precisely one-pointed concentration like this that allowed the Buddha-nature residing secretly within every single object and event in life to show itself. Yet Buddha-nature or no Buddha-nature, so far it was clearly more fun reading about the Zen of work than it was actually engaging in it.

Zen Pilgrimage

The thought of having to go through a kind of preparatory schooling did not deter me. I felt ready to go to any length if only there were some hope of my getting a bit nearer to Zen; and a roundabout way, however wearisome, seemed better to me than no way at all.

—EUGEN HERRIGEL

Much of Zen's influence on the West in recent decades has come from books written not by actual, bona fide, enlightened Zen masters, but by anxious, unenlightened Westerners trying against the odds to escape from a culture that they feel is no longer able to tell them the things they need to know. In the annals of the disaffected twentieth-century thinker's journey into intellectual lands unknown, Zen has been one of the great destinations. From bongo-playing, Benzedrine-addled Beats to armchair roshis like Alan Watts, to more responsible and serious-minded types like Gary Snyder, Peter Matthiessen, and Janwillem van de Wetering, the Western encounter with Zen has produced a great variety of first-person narratives. As a result, Zen enlightenment—the quintessential thing-you-can't-talk-about—now floats on a river of words a mile wide.

From the good to the bad and the profound to the silly, these adventures tend to unfold along similar lines. Fed up with modern life and all it entails, the Zen pilgrim sets off in search of a genuine alternative. He goes to Zen because he has inevitably heard that Zen practice offers an experience beyond the world of words and concepts that have now begun to bore and exhaust him so. Perhaps, like Fernando, this person has spent some time with both feet planted firmly in the world, giving life and all its pleasures the big Yes, and is now tired and disillusioned by the limitations of this path. Or perhaps like Nicky he has been trying to distance himself from worldly life and its distracting pleasures, but has found this route problematic, too. For someone in such a predicament, Zen holds out something beyond both the *via positiva* and the *via negativa*, as some of my more high-flying Life Manuals called the Path With Treats and the Path Without Treats. Neither ascetic nor indulgent, neither pessimistic nor optimistic, Zen hovers in the pilgrim's mind as a destination beyond all opposites, as well as beyond the eventual weariness of mind and body that goes with them. Zen offers enlightenment with no trimmings, and this is just the dish that the pilgrim now decides he wants. And so he sets off into the Zen landscape in the hopes that, like the hero in the famous series of ox-herding paintings, he can find the mysterious ox of enlightenment, make friends with it, and lead it back into the domain of his daily life.

It never goes easily. Typically, the Zen pilgrim finds a master, sets to work studying under him, but before too long finds his initial feelings of enthusiasm wearing off. This Zen stuff isn't any fun at all! Endless daily practice. Little or no results seen. Discouraging or downright humiliating reprimands from a master who day by day becomes more distant and harder to understand. The whole project seems not only more difficult than the ordinary life the pilgrim was trying so hard to escape from, but less honest, too, for though the rewards of ordinary life were perhaps unsatisfactory, they were at least *something*. The path the pilgrim has found himself on now, on the other hand, appears to lead nowhere at all.

Halfway into the story, the narrator tends to have reached a point where he is fed up with the whole business. This condition, however, turns out to be just the place the infuriatingly enigmatic Zen master has been waiting for him to get to. Knowing full well the deluded mental state his new pupil is in, the master has, through a numbing daily regimen of one sort or another, set out to change his thinking from inside out. The master may *appear* to be little more than a bossy, inscrutable, demanding jerk, but in fact this negative and abrasive persona was developed on purpose and is being used as a sort of psychological Brillo pad. The student's unconscious resistances to the ever-present and already-realized fact of sunyata—the simple, all-important truth that he or she has been enlightened the whole time but just didn't know it—have been breaking down silently and in secret.

Flashbulb Enlightenment

He drew his strong bow and invited me to step behind him and feel his arm muscles. They were indeed quite relaxed, as though they were doing no work at all.

—EUGEN HERRIGEL

Probably the single most influential Zen pilgrimage narrative is the German writer Eugen Herrigel's *Zen in the Art of Archery*, first published in English in 1953. Like many such books, it focuses not on Zen meditation per se but a specific art—in this case the seemingly simple act of shooting an arrow—that hides within itself the whole potential drama of enlightenment and its real- ization. Hungering for enlightenment, narrator Herrigel sets himself up with a Japanese archery master who proves to be the prototype for countless inscrutable masters of Zen pilgrimages to follow. Be one with the target. Let the arrow shoot itself. Never be pleased with your progress because when you are it's a sure sign you're off the mark. A whole catalog of such Life Manual clichés had their birth in Herrigel's little tale of Zen apprenticeship.

One of the biggest questions Herrigel wrestled with while spending month after month putting up with his obnoxiously inscrutable archery master was why everything had to take so *long*. If getting the hang of letting the arrow shoot itself and being one with the target was such a simple and thought-free affair, why did he have to waste day after day repeating the same tedious and simple-minded exercises? Eventually, Her- rigel learned the secret. All that time when he appeared not to be getting anywhere with his daily arrow exercises, he was really un-learning basic Western habits of thought that he had brought along to Japan with him—the chief of these being thinking that shooting an arrow was a transitive action, with shooter letting go of arrow and arrow hitting target. In truth, the whole process was not a matter of discrete elements acting upon one another in time, but a seamless event connected to all the other events in this vast, sunyata-based universe. It was pre- cisely Herrigel's ignorance of this—his certainty that there was some sort of separate person who needed to let go of the arrow at the right moment in order to hit a distant target—that had been preventing him from hitting it correctly all along.

Insight into sunyata, whether it comes via shooting arrows

at a target or some other seemingly mundane practice, takes a long time to achieve precisely because deep within us, something is resisting it. When this stubborn portion of our psyche that refuses to believe that all is one and all is empty finally falls away, enlightenment comes as easily, as Herrigel's archery master puts it at one point, as snow sliding off the branch of a tree. The secret of the art of Zen archery, like the secret of the art of Zen painting, or Zen flower arranging, or any other activity exalted or humble, lies in easing open the clenched fist of one's own mind. Once this is done, everything else takes care of itself.

Enlightenment on the Installment Plan

In Zen literature, a person's initial experience of sunyata (a moment sometimes referred to as kensho, a term that means roughly "seeing into one's true nature") can hit like a ton of bricks or brush like a feather. But however it comes, the writer who has finally achieved it tends to be aghast that he or she hadn't cottoned onto the experience much earlier. Countless Zen books provide tantalizing descriptions of this kensho moment, when, in a flash (the word *flash* appears often in these narratives), the world drops its guise of opacity and reveals its essential Buddha-nature. Self and other, mind and matter—all those tired old conceptual pairings shatter like wineglasses in the presence of a talented soprano. In one glorious moment, the all-too-familiar play of ordinary life is over. Or rather, it isn't *really* over, because everything keeps going on just as it was before. The only difference is that now everything has Buddha-nature and all people are Buddhas—totally enlightened, perfect in all their flawed particularity, in need of nothing.

For someone who absorbs enough literature on this marvelous moment when the wrecking ball of sunyata shatters the tiresome old housing project of mundane consciousness, the question inevitably arises as to whether there might not be a shortcut to it. For just as there seem to be individuals in the Adult Unlike Other Adults address book who can be enlightened without having to give up worldly pleasures of one sort or another, so also are there those who cotton onto enlightenment with very little stress or struggle. It's sensible enough that this would be the case, considering the fact that "getting enlightened" really just means realizing that you actually have always been so. If in truth there isn't any work to do or any workers to do it, if everyone really is enlightened already and just doesn't know it, all those months or years of gruesomely dull practice that writers like Herrigel describe might be necessary for some people, but not for all of them.

One of the more plucky illustrations of this idea came to me around this time from D. E. Harding, author of a Zen Life Manual with the engaging title *On Having No Head.* Harding actually had the audacity to compare enlightenment to an appliance that can be purchased outright or on credit. Some people, Harding explained, slave away at various spiritual practices for years and years to achieve enlightenment. Others, meanwhile, have it drop on them more or less out of the blue. Keeping the enlightenment experience fresh once you get it always takes work, Harding cautioned. But why couldn't getting one's initial insight, or kensho, be like buying an item on credit and paying it off later? To keep your initial experience of sunyata fresh, you just had to make your "payments" of diligent Zen practice—but to get it in the first place did not necessarily mean long months or even years of toil and boredom. The flashbulb could go off any old time.

Be Here Now

Traveling is a fool's paradise. We owe to our first journeys the discovery that place is nothing. At home I dream that at Naples, at Rome, I can be intoxicated with beauty and lose my sadness. I pack my trunk, embrace my friends, embark on the sea and at last wake up in Naples, and there beside me is the stern Fact, the sad Self, unrelenting, identical, that I fled from. I seek the Vatican and the palaces. I affect to be intoxicated with sights and suggestions, but I am not intoxicated. My giant goes with me wherever I go.

—EMERSON

It didn't take a long time on the road for Harding's notion of enjoy-now-pay-later enlightenment to start sounding a lot better to me than Herrigel's earn-it-first version. Just as I had begun to suspect it would, chronicling the country visually turned out to be an arduous and tiresome process, and getting a Zen-type relationship going with Nicky's lenses and film canisters as we schlepped from one sleepy Colombian town to another soon started to seem like a fantastically far-fetched idea. With all the traveling to be done there was little time to refer back to my Life Manuals in order to keep the details of what I was supposed to be accomplishing straight in my head, and before long my high-flying notions of transforming camera-caddying into an enlightenment-inducing Zen practice were a distant memory.

The big difference between Zen and the Tibetan Buddhism that Nicky was putting into practice turned out to lie in the details of approach rather than in essential doctrine. Enlightenment was the thing to be had in Tibetan Buddhism just as it was in Zen, the catch being that the Tibetan variety was a good bit more stodgy in its insistence on actually doing things like meditating and studying in order to obtain this result. Flashy notions such as Harding's awaken-now-pay-later model of enlightenment were in distinctly short supply in the few books on the subject Nicky had brought along with him, and the utilitarian focus in them often struck me as distressingly dreary. Getting enlightened seemed to take an awfully long time in the world of Tibetan Buddhism (in fact, more than a single human incarnation most of the time) and to require an awful lot of work as well. There was something relentlessly *sensible* about the whole business—at least in comparison to some of my peppier Zen manuals.

After a while I began to figure out that, for all that it put me off, this sensible quality was precisely what had attracted Nicky to begin with. He had always been a fastidious, quality-conscious type, and it was easy to see how such a super-sensible style of Buddhism could appeal to a person who, back in his materialist days, always sought out the best-made and most long-lasting products, who had always filled out and sent in the proper warranties, and who, from clothes to cameras, always kept everything properly cleaned, properly oiled, and properly polished, as the case may be. Tibetan Buddhism fit perfectly with such a sensibility, for its attractiveness, like that of a Swiss Army knife or a pair of German hiking boots, derived from its functional efficiency. Unlike with Zen, that efficiency did not necessarily imply spareness or streamlinedness. Just as a Swiss Army knife could be an inch thick with blades and tools, so, too, was Tibetan Buddhism full of all kinds of complicated doctrines and practices, and even gods and goddesses. Yet beneath them all, there always lay that deep and all-pervasive atmosphere of the sensible and the practical.

Quality-conscious sort that he was, Nicky must have been sorely tested at times by his new assistant—for though he did his best to be patient with me, I continued to be less than stellar at most of the tasks assigned. I still felt no particular Zen kinship with that enormous camera of his, and as I wrestled it off and on one cramped Colombian bus after another, my zest for the adventure dwindled steadily. Not only was there hard work to do and long hours of relative discomfort to endure: there was also a pesky feeling of the futility of the whole project. Apparently it took more than just travel to escape from the sensation that life doesn't make much sense. A general atmosphere of pointlessness was going on here, in the far-flung mountain villages and steamy equatorial plains that Nicky and I bumped and dragged through, just as it was back on the East Coast. Crowded into this or that bus with a mixed bag of laborers, mothers and children, chickens, goats, and the occasional pair of stoned, blank-faced German tourists, I found myself presented with evermore unwanted lessons in the art of being comfortable with the Moment. The heat, the fumes, the clucking of the chickens, and perhaps worst of all the endless salsa music that blasted out of the primitive, high-treble speakers these buses always seemed to be outfitted with: it all went to show that at most, I had only discovered a slightly different flavor of discontent, tedium, and pointlessness down here in the tropics than the one that ruled back home.

I knew, in a perverse kind of way, that if I was somewhere else, reading about myself rumbling along a Colombian dirt road at the back of a bus, slightly nauseated from some bad water drunk the night before and with salsa music boring into my skull like a dentist's drill, the whole experience would be quite interesting. It was actually *being there* that was the problem, and despite how many of my Life Manuals emphasized the importance of plunging into the moment, I just couldn't seem to do it.

Of course, it wasn't so bad all the time. Many of the towns we visited were pleasant and interesting in one way or another, and even the rattier ones had a charm and humanity that I was not sufficiently spoiled and self-preoccupied to miss completely. But the underlying lesson for me as I trailed after Nicky was that there was something—some key to this business of just being where you were and doing what you were doing— that I still didn't get.

To Judge or Not to Judge

Patience is a quality of heart that can be greatly enhanced with deliberate practice.

—RICHARD CARLSON, PH.D., *DON'T SWEAT THE SMALL STUFF . . . AND IT'S ALL SMALL STUFF*

There were other factors at work as well. Far too wrapped up in myself to have a coherent social conscience, I did at least manage to have an incoherent one, and what that conscience now told me was that there was something slightly grotesque about what we were up to. Most of the villages we traveled through were desperately poor, and everywhere in them a battle was going on: a battle between the old and the new, between the traditional and the synthetic, between the pretty and the nasty looking. Capsized car bodies, disposable diapers, plastic food and drink containers—for some reason this endless drift of brightly colored modern crap was ten times more noticeable amid the lush Colombian landscape than it was back in the States. Where, exactly, did a pair of first-world dandies like us get off traipsing around a third-world country drowning in all this industrial junk and corruption, taking pictures of it?

Thanks to his Buddhist equanimity, Nicky was largely able to avoid this question. Being a Buddhist photographer meant recording the bad and the good without judgment, so though he noticed all the nasty stuff just as much as I did and probably even more, it never seemed to drag him down as much as it sometimes did me. After all, the whole *point* of Nicky's Buddhism was that it acknowledged that the world was full of pain, misery, ugliness, and injustice: that's why he was working so hard at getting unattached to it in the first place. It was me, with my ambiguous feelings about the *via positiva* and the *via negativa*, and which of the two I was better off heading down, who had the real trouble accepting all the depressing stuff we saw in the course of our travels.

Six weeks or so into the adventure, and sometime after the combined forces of existential indirection and first-world guilt were really starting to get the better of me, Nicky received some information that put a bright new spin on things. It turned out that one of Paco's friends knew of a genuine Indian shaman who was willing to be photographed, and he was relatively easy to reach as well. An actual sorcerer! After struggling to apply the lens of cool Zen equanimity both to myself and to my troublesome surroundings, and failing at it for such a long time, an encounter with a romantic figure of this kind sounded like just the thing to restore my enthusiasm.

Needless to say, actually meeting a genuine "man of knowledge," as Castaneda referred to the Native American wise men in his books, violated what was becoming an unspoken rule about keeping all interactions with the Adult Unlike Other Adults confined to the pages of my Life Manuals. What if I was disappointed? I also knew from Castaneda's books that the world was thick with phony Indian shamans, and that finding a real one was a matter not only of long research but of great luck as well. Don Juan had told Carlos many times that a true sorcerer never allowed his image to be captured on film, so it was a bit suspicious that this one was apparently so willing to see us. Still, don Juan lived up in the Sonora Desert. Perhaps the rules about such things were different down here. And maybe if this shaman *was* real, actually laying eyes on him might work some sort of transformational magic on me, such as my daily regimen of camera maintenance so clearly wasn't. Even if I *was* growing more and more timid about the prospect of actually encountering a genuine wisdom figure in flesh and blood and three dimensions, it was obvious that such an attitude would not benefit me in the long run. Better to nip the tendency in the bud if possible—and here, perhaps, was just the chance to do so.

Meeting a Sorcerer

Don Juan and Carlos's adventures were much on my mind on the morning when Nicky and I—after the usual endless bus rides and a final journey by hired Jeep through a vast, anonymous stretch of lowland jungle—stood before a primitive, one-room house in a remote village. It turned out that the owner of the house—a tiny man with a broad, pleasant face dressed in worn blue dungarees and a T-shirt—was not the shaman we were looking for but a friend of his. This was not too surprising, as I knew that when Carlos was looking for sorcerers without don Juan's help, it was always a long process of driving here and there and back again, talking to one person and another and another. To find a genuine Adult Unlike Other Adults in one step, you usually had to have one of them along with you; otherwise, plenty of patience was necessary.

Nicky and our driver worked out some more details about the real shaman's whereabouts, and we got back in the Jeep and traveled deeper into the jungle. After another long, bumpy drive through moist air and an endless expanse of surplus-store green, the Jeep brought us to another village, this one even smaller and sleepier than the first. At first nobody seemed to be around. There weren't even any of the thin, skittish dogs that were so depressingly common in most of the towns and villages. After our driver turned off the Jeep's engine, however, I realized we were not alone after all. Noise was coming from the house the driver had stopped in front of—in fact, quite a bit of it. The three of us hopped out and approached the house's single, half-open doorway. Considering the remoteness of the location, I found it odd that no one had come out to greet the sound of the Jeep, and it now became clear that our presence had gone unnoticed because something really hilarious was going on inside. The little house—again composed of only a single room—seemed almost to shake with wild laughter.

Our guide entered, and Nicky and I, ducking our heads, followed. It was quite dark, but I could see well enough to notice that the place was strangely short on furniture. The only major object in the room was a long wooden bench set against one wall. The floor was dirt, with a space of a few inches open between it and the walls all the way around. The walls themselves were free of decoration save for the one opposite the bench, at the center of which hung a page that looked like it had been torn from an American magazine. The face in the picture was familiar, but it took a moment for me to figure out who it was. Shaun Cassidy—the younger brother of *Partridge Family* star David, who had recently had a hit on the charts in the States. What was Shaun Cassidy's face doing here, on the wall of this house, in the heart of this sweaty, anonymous jungle? I didn't have time to ponder the question, for there were more details to take in and analyze. Perhaps the most suggestive and troublesome of these was the sweet yet nasty smell that filled the place—a smell I identified, after a moment, as oxidizing alcohol.

On the bench sat two men, somewhere in their fifties or sixties, dressed, as the man in the previous village had been, in dungarees and T-shirts. Both held small plastic cups in their hands, and on the ground before them was a bottle of something called aguardiente. I recognized the stuff because I had seen it everywhere on our trips. Made from pressed sugarcane and exceptionally inexpensive, the stuff was Tres Esquinas's only real competition for Colombia's alcoholic beverage of choice. On the side of the room opposite the two men, seated cross-legged on the dirt floor with a cup of her own, was a woman dressed in a plain, somewhat grubby cotton shift who looked a little older, and a little drunker, than the men. The three of them stared over at us, the subject of their laughter seemingly forgotten. There was a moment of awkward silence. Finally the woman, pointing to us, said something in a loud, raspy, incomprehensible Spanish to her two friends. Then the three of them exploded into laughter again.

When it had died down a bit, our guide engaged one of the men in conversation. I tried to follow what was going on but soon gave up. Nicky, however, was listening carefully, and in a moment he spoke to me in a low voice.

"He's telling them why we're here. That one on the left is the shaman."

The shaman, who, Zen acceptance or no Zen acceptance, didn't look at all the way I had wanted him to, listened as our guide spoke his piece. Then he nodded his head slowly and gravely and barked out a few sentences. Again the guide turned and spoke to Nicky, and Nicky spoke to me.

"Maybe we can take his picture," Nicky said, "but we have to sit with them first for a while so they can get to know us."

"Get to know us! They're not even going to remember we were here by tomorrow morning. Let's just get out of here."

As if he hadn't heard me at all, Nicky went over and sat down between the two men. I considered my options, but realized I didn't have many, as the old woman was now gesturing for me to come sit by her. Slowly but surely getting more angry, I walked over and plunked down on the ground next to her, whereupon she gave me a friendly whack on the back and offered me a drink from her plastic cup. I smiled weakly and shook my head. She then embarked on a dense and extraordinarily rapid monologue, not a word of which could I understand.

Over on the bench Nicky was getting the same treatment from the two men, but he was clearly having a better time of it than I was, thanks, as usual, to his infuriating Buddhist patience. If up until now Nicky's ability to be in the Moment without succumbing to judgment or scorn was something I had regarded with puzzled respect, I now felt suddenly quite ready to strangle him for it. To hell with him, I thought to myself. To hell with being in the Moment, and to hell with the Buddha, and Zen, and the camera in the Jeep outside, and this whole lousy, tragic, stupid, worn-out, broken-down, irritating, garbage-filled world we were dragging it through. To hell with it all. For some mysterious reason, my disappointed expectations were producing a sensation of self-loathing that was just as strong as the one I felt for everything and everyone else. What a spoiled, naive jerk I had been, expecting to find some romantic Man of Knowledge waiting for me here in this all-too-ordinary jungle.

Nicky's Spanish was fairly good, and in response to this or that statement he would nod his head, smile patiently, and say a few words in reply. Perhaps to escape from the still all-but-overpowering smell of alcohol, and also no doubt to keep an eye on the equipment, our guide had stepped back out of the hut and into the overcast daylight. Through the doorway I could see him, standing by the Jeep, smoking a Pielroja. Though completely one-sided save for the occasional nod or "*no comprendo*" from me, my conversation with the old woman ground on for a good fifteen minutes. Occasionally I would attempt a withering glance over at Nicky, but he either didn't want to acknowledge me or was actually caught up in the conversation he was having with the two men. At long last, the three of them got to their feet and I took the opportunity to get up, too.

"What's going on?"

"He's agreed to let me photograph him," Nicky said, even-toned and again completely devoid of sarcasm.

"That's terrific. Anthropologists around the world are going to be grateful for your efforts."

Again Nicky said nothing in return but exited the house behind the two men. Meanwhile the woman, who had moved over to the bench the men had left, refilled her plastic cup and gestured for me to join her. I smiled and motioned apologetically to the doorway, suggesting that my efforts were needed outside. When I stepped out into the light, Nicky and the guide were unloading our gear from the Jeep, the shaman's Indian friend was standing and watching them vacantly, and the shaman himself was nowhere to be seen. A few children, dressed in the usual brightly colored Western textiles, had emerged from the other huts, and I realized the little village hadn't been so empty after all.

"Where's the shaman?" I said.

"Over there in one of those huts," said Nicky, passing the main camera bag to me. "He needs to change into his costume. Do you have the cash I gave you this morning?"

"Yeah. Why?"

"We need to pay him."

"Pay him! Oh, come on. Don't tell me you're really considering giving this guy money, too?"

Nicky remained maddeningly unwilling to share in or even acknowledge my irritation. He really was riding this stupid nonjudgment horse to the end of the race. I found the cash and gave it to him, and in a few moments more the shaman emerged from a nearby hut. Though still drunk, he was now dressed up in a surprisingly dramatic native outfit, including an elaborate feather headdress and what seemed to be a sort of magician's staff, also outfitted with a couple of feathers. Even though I continued to despise him, I had to admit he looked pretty impressive. Nicky directed him to stand over by the house, and we commenced our usual camera-setup drill. As we did so, ever more villagers, adults and children, appeared from here and there and watched the process.

Nicky's camera worked best with long exposures, and he now explained the need to hold very still to the shaman, who cooperated as best he could, staring ferociously at Nicky's lens and trying not to sway back and forth too much. Occasionally, as if to help himself stay in character, he produced a short, angry grunt and shook his magician's staff menacingly.

I stood in my usual spot behind Nicky as he hunched under the old-fashioned black photographer's cloak and fiddled with the knobs of his complicated camera. There before us, in one neat package, stood the whole Life Manual problem. It was a problem I had now become fairly good at reading and thinking about, but which I was not a whit better at approaching and actually dealing with in real life than I had been when I first started addressing it more than a year before. The world, said my Life Manuals, was not what I wanted it to be. In fact, it was quite often just about the absolute opposite of that, down to the smallest detail. But if I was to take the basic Life Manual program of action seriously, I was not to be put off by this fact. Instead, I was to learn how to see the world as perfect and lacking for nothing, even for all that it might not seem to be so. In order to do this, I needed to apply the Brillo pad of nonjudgment to all my accustomed habits and perceptions. I needed to act, to work, to think, and to observe, and I needed to do so without ever asking things to be other than just as they were. If I did this long enough—and perhaps even if I did it for just a short while—the world, or my perception of it, would eventually change. I would see, to my great joy and surprise, that everything really *was* just as it was supposed to be, and always had been.

In a few minutes Nicky was satisfied and we packed up the camera. After a little more conversation and the passing over of some money, we got back in the Jeep and drove away, with the shaman and his two friends and some of the other villagers waving us off. Nicky had the shots he wanted—shots not of ideal, romanticized reality, but of the flawed, frustrating, determinedly ordinary reality that life specializes in. If I was ever to be happy with that reality myself, it was clear that I still had plenty more work to do.

CHAPTER 5

THE PATH OF THE ARTIST

Good-bye to Colombia

But life is also an art, and the man who would become a con-
summate artist in living must follow, on all levels of his being,
the same procedure as that by which the painter or the sculp-
tor or any other craftsman comes to his own more limited
perfection.

—ALDOUS HUXLEY

Not too long after our adventure with the drunken shaman,
Nicky and I packed up the big camera once and for all and
returned to the States. Selling the photography project as a
book had not worked out so far; Nicky had things back in New
York he needed to attend to, and I was about ready to give the
Zen of work a break—at least in the manner I had been trying
it so far. I was still set on getting enlightened, of course—and
the faster the better—but it was starting to look like a smarter
idea to pursue this project without cutting myself off from the

world in quite so radical a fashion as I had been doing. Once I had made the unfortunate discovery that geographical distance does not in itself make one's life more exotic or interesting, Colombia's remoteness had increasingly come to feel like a drawback. It was time to return from this blazing hot Martian backwater to the familiar East Coast, time to see Elena again, and time also to redouble my efforts at figuring out where exactly, between the extremes of the *via positiva* followed by people like Fernando, and the *via negativa* followed by people like Nicky, my own particular path to genuine wisdom lay.

Stuck Between Plus and Minus

Once you have given up the ghost, everything follows with dead certainty, even in the midst of chaos.

—HENRY MILLER

There was no question that I was having more and more suspicions about the *via negativa* option. Living day to day with a genuine Buddhist had by now made me deeply doubtful about my chances of successfully approaching the world and all its problems along Buddhist lines. The problem was not that Nicky was betraying the impossibility of this route—that under scrutiny he was turning out to be a mere poseur. Rather, the more time we spent together, the more I could see how genuine he was about taking the Buddha's life recommendations seriously. What ended up bugging me about Nicky's new life as a Buddhist was precisely the fact that he *was* so successful at it. As the weeks out in the bush piled up, I continued to find it strangely vexing that he managed to flow with the day-to-day details so much better than I did, despite his being so convinced that from a larger perspective neither he nor I nor anyone else really existed—at least in any ultimate sense. Having said No to life really seemed to have made Nicky better able to chronicle its mingled beauties and uglinesses without judgment or expectation. Meanwhile I—who couldn't seem to muster up such an unequivocal view—floundered hopelessly in just the sea of desires, expectations, judgments, and disappointments that Nicky was leaving behind.

Nicky's attitude toward the world and all its attractions and repulsions extended even to photography itself—as I discovered by watching, week by week, the curious combination of affection and suspicion he showed for his camera and the process of taking pictures in general. Was Nicky's Buddhism so unrelentingly severe that he even had to consider chucking photography—the skill he most liked and was most accomplished at—in the garbage as well? Not necessarily, Nicky explained. Attachment to one's craft was no different from attachment to pleasure or power or anything else. Photography wasn't "bad"—but what *was* bad was getting dependent on it—allowing its various gratifications to feed the nonexistent ego and strengthen it in the disastrous illusion that it did in fact exist and was in fact important. Hence photography, for all that he might love it, was potentially as much a danger to his true path as anything else might be.

The more time I spent following Nicky around as he gingerly made his way through the minefield of potential attachments that the world had now become for him, the more I realized that my own attitude toward life and all the things in it was not going to be resolved until I gave it a good solid shove in a definite direction. Unfortunately, just because I seemed unable to go completely in the direction of saying No to life as Nicky had did not mean that I was able to say Yes to it instead. I may have been no Nicky, with his calm, considered, slightly melancholy assurance that all phenomena—even photography itself—were little more than potential sources of attachment and pain, but I was no Fernando either. For as lovable as Fernando was with his perpetual self-assurance and his giddy, substance-fueled determination to see life as a totally *chévere* event from top to bottom, I was far from being able to duplicate such an attitude myself.

It was hard to know which was more confusing: the mingled desires and doubts I felt toward the world around me or the similarly ambivalent feelings that arose when I turned my gaze in the opposite direction and focused on my inner self—a self that, Nicky and my Zen texts to the contrary, certainly *felt* real enough as it continued to undergo all the endless attractions, repulsions, enthusiasms, and misgivings that made up my daily experience.

Positive and Negative at the Same Time

During our final weeks at my father's house, with no more Life Manuals of my own left, I took to fulfilling my wisdom-reading requirements by scavenging among the small library of sun-bleached paperbacks left behind by previous visitors. Among these were a few books by someone named Henry Miller, a writer I had never encountered before, but whom my father's caretaker Paco recommended without reservation. Miller's books, Paco reported, had changed his life when he first read them in his early twenties—and were renowned for having had the same effect on many other people. Without their influence, Paco might never have said good-bye to his life in America and come down here to Colombia to start his restaurant. Paco's recommendation was enough to get me to read the books seriously, and to my surprise I soon found in them just the new set of clues to help me get out of the dead area between the two poles of the *via positiva* and the *via negativa* where I had been lingering so long.

Writing wasn't just a means of communicating ideas or stories for Miller—it was an entire style of being in the world. Far from viewing his craft as an "attachment" and keeping it at arm's length, he had plunged so deep into it that the old Miller—the person he had presumably been before he became a writer—had disappeared altogether. Like most of the other "artistic" characters I had met so far, whether in real life or on paper, Miller was clearly a rather enormous egotist. In fact, all he really liked to talk about was himself, and even when he was talking about other people it was always clear that he was doing so within the specific context of what *he* thought about them. But he somehow managed to pull off this self-preoccupation in a way that made it excusable, and even admirable. Miller's egotism was so determinedly huge that it was almost as if he had no ego at all.

The Artist of Life

So far in my Life Manual journey, I had consistently been presented with a series of choices. Love yourself or deny yourself. Engage with the world or retreat from the world. Celebrate desire and pleasure or combat them at every step. And also so far, the most intriguing Life Manual characters I had encountered were those who—like Lao-tzu and Arjuna and some of those crazy Zen painters—somehow managed to combine these opposite choices into a single package. Miller now introduced me to the most convincing incarnation of this figure yet: a magically paradoxical person who managed to say both Yes and No to life at the same time, and who did so by means of creativity—of art.

When Miller talked about artists, I could tell that he meant something more by the term than just someone who put paint on a canvas or words on a page. Miller's ideal artist, it was plain to see, was an Artist of Life, and that meant that while this person usually had a manuscript or a studio full of pictures to show for himself, he might easily not have any solid evidence of his special grasp of life other than his unique and marvelous personality. Whether Miller spoke of writers and painters and sculptors from times past or of people he knew personally, it was clear that he himself had no doubts about the actual existence of this marvelous species of human being. As Miller sketched his outlines from one angle after another, I knew for sure that I had blundered into yet another incarnation of the Adult Unlike Other Adults—and that this version might just be the most vivid and fruitful one I had encountered yet.

Devouring the World

The first word any man writes when he has found himself, his own rhythm, which is the life rhythm, is Yes! Everything he writes thereafter is Yes, Yes, Yes—Yes in a thousand million ways. No dynamo, no matter how huge—not even a dynamo of a hundred million dead souls—can combat one man saying Yes!

—HENRY MILLER

Primitive and childlike yet at the same time infinitely sophisticated, Miller's Artist of Life had been transformed by the world's maddening contradictions into an equally contradictory creature. He was "the most active of men and yet serene as a lama." He was "tender and ruthless at the same time." He was "the crude ore from which the finest of metals are made." Such artists, said Miller, were often none too successful from a material perspective, but living in cold-water tenements and scrounging just to get by didn't bother them a bit because their commitment to aggressively accepting *all* of life made them comfortable in the world in a way that an ordinary person couldn't even begin to understand. In some paradoxical way, even being *uncomfortable* was comfortable to them.

The big secret of Miller's Artist of Life was that he was engaged with life in a unique kind of way. Seeking neither to cure himself of desire for the things of the world, nor wasting too much time greedily chasing them around, he used all the experience that came his way as grist for a mysterious transformational process that went on constantly within himself. The Artist of Life knew as well as the bleakest Buddhist that even at its best life was a matter not so much of pleasure but of pain. But rather than spurning life because of this, or futilely trying to separate out the good parts from the bad, the Artist of Life gobbled *all* of life down with the determined gusto of a contender in a pie-eating contest.

Much like Arjuna and the Taoist sages I had begun my Life Manual studies with, Miller's ideal artist was entirely ready to plunge into the muck of life—but he did so in a manner that struck me as decidedly more *modern*. Where my venerable Taoists had been largely content to let things be, to float along in the great cosmic drift and disintegrate altogether if the weather dictated that they do so, the Artist of Life was more concerned with charging actively through the world as a distinct and definite personality. Unlike Fernando—who, I realized, was close to but not quite one of these figures himself—Miller's artist knew full well that the world was really a not-so-*chévere* place at all. But rather than simply pretend that it was, he plunged deep into all the garbage and darkness around him, and used the stuff he encountered as raw material for the all-important creative process. Whatever he saw and whatever happened to him, from the great to the good to the absolutely lousy, became fuel for the vast smoky furnace that burned perpetually inside him. By attacking life with this omnivorously creative attitude, he could transform even the most unpleasant experience into something positive. The works of art themselves—be they books or paintings or sculptures made from coat hangers—were almost an incidental by-product of this process.

Getting to the End of the Rope

Oddly enough, a key part of becoming one of these Milleresque artists was being thoroughly beaten by life—of coming, as Miller put it, to the end of your rope. Despite the fact that the Artist of Life was in some ways the most gargantuan of egomaniacs, in another way he was more humble than the most selfless ascetic, because his ego had been *transformed* by the trials and tribulations of his life. Again and again Miller described the basic process. Your typical genuine artist had a long history of trying to make a go of it in life. He had tried to earn a living, tried to secure fame and respect, tried to become happy, tried to find love—and had failed miserably at all of it. Eventually, he hit a point where so much failure and disappointment piled up that he was forced to throw up his hands and surrender. Done in by the world and all its demands, he walked about as a dead man for a time. Then, gradually—astonishingly—this death turned into a new sort of life. Having thrown all his old ideas about success and happiness out the window, he found himself entering back into life with a new energy and a strange new assurance. And as he did so, works of art of one sort or another flowed from his hands without cease.

I Reach a Career Choice

With a weird, mesmerizing authority, Miller pitched the notion of salvation and enlightenment through art as I had never heard it pitched before, and as usual, I swallowed it hook, line, and sinker. Miller, being himself one of these reborn artistic individuals, had followed the same pattern of growth-through-suffering that he described taking place for others. After struggling for years to write a Great Work, he had finally given up all hope of doing so—and it was only then that his Muse (as Miller sometimes called that higher, better part of himself where all his true creativity lay) started speaking to him. And how she spoke! At his best, Miller informed me, his material was whispered direct from the Muse's mouth into his ear, and all he had to do at these times was type down the words as they came.

This last bit sounded especially good. Having never been all that sure of what I wanted to do in life, yet grimly aware that everyone had to do something, I now hit upon writing as the perfect solution to my dilemma—the perfect way of blending activity and inactivity, egotism and egolessness, acceptance of the world and disdain for it, into one fantastical sandwich.

Write Your Way to Wisdom

Be alert, always, for the presence of the Great Creator leading and helping your artist.

—JULIA CAMERON, *THE ARTIST'S WAY*

With our return to America and the conclusion of my camera-caddying duties coming up, that problem of what to do with myself was once again looming before me—and the idea of sitting down at a typewriter and having words whoosh out onto the page was an extremely appealing solution. Writing my way to enlightenment would combine all the best elements of the life recipes I had studied so far. It had some of Taoism's emphasis on effortlessness, some of the Zen technique of combining contrasting elements into a paradoxical unity, and not a little of the Bhagavad Gita's can-do, action-is-all attitude as well—

though without, apparently, the necessity of actually going anywhere or doing anything. Rather than traipsing here and there around the globe, trying to figure out how to be an Adult Unlike Other Adults in exotic and inconvenient locations, I could come to terms with the world and all its contradictions from the comfort of a single writing desk.

Not that minor logistical details didn't remain. After all, sitting at a writing desk obviously entailed actual writing, and my experiences with this activity thus far in my life had not been especially fun or even pleasant. Writing was only the liberating, freewheeling, transformative process Miller described it to be once one had broken through into a condition of unhampered creative lucidity—once one had come to the end of one's rope and been magically reborn as a genuine Artist of Life. How, I wondered, did one get quickly to this place where the Muse spilled the beans on command and writing was a free and easy process rather than a pinched and tortured task? If being an Artist of Life meant getting broken down and remade by living and all the crap that went along with it, had I been through a sufficient amount of this sort of thing yet in my short and, at least for the moment, extremely privileged life, or was I going to have to suffer for decades like Miller had, struggling just to get by, laboring at nasty low-end jobs, cranking out ream after ream of bad, uninspired writing? I could, if I wished, brace myself for decades of struggle, but as usual my hopes were high that a softer, easier way might be found. Surely, if I approached it with the right attitude, the trick of getting the dope straight from the Muse's mouth might come a little quicker for me than it had for others.

Next Stop: Creativity

It was now late spring, and back in the States my stepmother's house out on Long Island lay idle. Once he got back to New

York, Nicky was planning on returning to his humble Buddhist digs in the city and coming out to this house on weekends. My father and stepmother might be passing through now and then as well, but by and large I could have the place to myself. Away from all distractions, with no cameras to carry or college classes to worry about, I could use the endless empty hours to put Miller's fascinating proposition of engagement-with-life-through-writing to the test.

Very likely, the first days of this regimen would be tedious in the extreme. After all, the Muse had let Miller toil away for actual *decades* with no success, so it was unlikely that I was going to get off without an initial dry period. But thanks to my faith in Miller's tantalizing description of the transformative possibilities hidden within the creative process, I continued to hope that getting to this goal might go at least somewhat quickly. Our final days in Colombia were full of happy expectation on my part. Now when Fernando, on his afternoon visits to our house, grabbed my shoulders and repeated the familiar news that everything was *chévere*, I would nod my head with a little more assurance. For now I knew that though the world wasn't, in fact, really such a *chévere* place at all, the path of the Artist of Life that I was now embarking on would lead me to a condition in which, for the first time, I might really be able to accept and make use of this fact.

Breaking Through to the Wisdom Within

You must be a great warrior when you contact first thoughts and write them down.

—NATALIE GOLDBERG, *WRITING DOWN THE BONES*

After a brief stop at my parents' house in Virginia (my sister and brother-in-law had moved away in the interim), I traveled up to

Philadelphia to see how college was coming along for Elena, and to establish where our relationship, such as it was, now stood after my long absence. To my dismay, I had found myself moping over Elena quite a bit down in the tropics, and the melancholy her absence engendered had served as the basis for many a talk with Nicky about love, sex, and other attachment-related issues. Seeing her again now—and finding that she was happy to see me, too—was both a relief and a fresh source of concern. For in my absence, Elena seemed to have grown even more purposeful about her life than she had been before. Her classes had become more, not less, interesting, and she now had many, many friends, all of whom also seemed to be plugged into some general switchboard of conventional adult concerns I had no clue about. The world economy, President Reagan's performance, the new lecture series on urban design: there seemed to be no limit to the ordinary, sensible topics Elena and her friends were willing to discuss. Into this crowd I fit about as well as a mastodon on a mink farm, and though it was clear that Elena was prepared to expend the effort to make me feel comfortable anyhow, it was not so clear whether I was willing to accept that effort from her.

When, after a few days, I headed north to Long Island to commence my self-imposed creative exile, it was with both sadness at leaving Elena again, and a certain relief at escaping the hyperadjusted world she now inhabited. Once out on Long Island, I found myself stationed just where I had planned to be—at a desk in a guest room on the second floor of my stepmother's house, a pad of paper in front of me and nothing but time to feel my way into that mysterious process of creation that Miller had set as my task of the moment.

Questions of the all-knowing Muse aside, what, exactly, was I intending to write? I didn't really know, but I suspected that it would be a book of some sort—one similar, most likely, to the Life Manuals I so loved to read. Of course, I wasn't foolish enough to think that the normal, everyday "me" had any great wisdom about life to share, but this didn't matter because the path of the artist dictated that any idiot could come up with worthwhile material if he really surrendered to the creative process—if he was *real* about what he was doing. The trick seemed to be to realize that everyone was really much wiser than they knew, but that in most people most of the time, this wisdom was off-limits. Though everybody was potentially in touch with all the wisdom they could possibly want right within themselves, it lay stacked up behind closed doors. Surrendering wholeheartedly to the creative process, however, could—if done properly—break down these doors and make this material accessible. Indeed, if you really succeeded in hacking your way through to this normally unavailable creativity stockpile, the big problem was simply writing fast enough to get it all down.

Thus, as unlikely as it might have seemed, I knew now that somewhere within me lay a book: a real book that, once I had written it, would run through multiple printings and change all sorts of people in all sorts of wonderful ways. Readers all around the globe would stumble upon it just as I had stumbled upon Miller's battered paperbacks and receive from its pages a strong dose of much-needed news about the real deal with life and how best to go about living it. Speaking from a place of wisdom and authority far beyond the reach of my ordinary, everyday consciousness, I would gain membership, through having written this book, in that small, wild brotherhood of genuine Adults Unlike Other Adults—the people whom I had for so long been admiring yet having such a tough time meeting in three dimensions. My life, having broken down the door separating me from my higher, wiser self and having

learned as well how to take dictation from it, would be transformed into an altogether more relaxed and fluid affair than it
had been so far. As the author of this marvelous Book Among
Books, I could go where I wanted and do what I would. The
point would not be that I had secured fame or fortune through
it, for these were, of course, trifling matters. What *would* be
important was that, having blazed a trail to my higher and better self, I would from then on always be able to turn to that self,
in moments of confusion or despair, and get all the answers I
needed.

Waiting for the Muse

When a few days had come and gone and the Muse hadn't
shown up, I didn't think too much of it. After all, if Miller had
been able to wait actual decades before *Tropic of Cancer* blasted
out of him like water from a long-dry spigot, the least I could
do was give the process a week or two. But oh, how the time
dragged. Before long Nicky—now back in his routine as a free-
lance photographer in the city—came out with some friends of
his, relaxing after a week of work. What a cheerful bunch they
were—and why shouldn't they be! Having spent five days actually doing something, they had all earned the right to unwind
from the process. For me, however, not having wound myself
up with any actual labor other than staring at that blank writing
tablet, unwinding was not an available option. Sunday came
and went, Nicky and his friends returned to the city, and I was
once again looking at five more structureless, Muse-free days—
days in which the nice house I was in, the beautiful ocean
nearby, the full refrigerator, and all the time in the world to find
myself through art were harshly compromised by the fact that
I had nothing to say and no way of saying it. To my horror,

enlightenment-through-creativity was proving just as tough a prospect as enlightenment by any other method.

From Small Self to Big Self

There are two natures, one self-existent, and the other ever in want.

—PLATO

Wisdom wouldn't be wisdom if it wasn't—at least potentially—available to everybody. Likewise, the path of wisdom-through-creativity wouldn't be the popular option it has become in recent years—through books like *Writing Down the Bones* and *The Artist's Way*—without the assertion that everyone has, somewhere within them, the potential to genuinely transform themselves through the creative act. Whether they spell it out in such terms or not, most of the new breed of creativity manuals base their strategies of releasing the artist within on the old and venerable idea—central to many a wisdom tradition—that each person has essentially two selves: a higher, larger, better one and a smaller, lower, not-so-good one.

Whiny, needy, ever on the lookout for pleasure, compliments, and other reassuring feedback, the small self—also known in many Life Manuals these days as the ego—is a creature that needs little introduction for most people, for most of us spend most of our time stuck within its confines. Nor does the larger, better self described by these doctrines need much introduction either, for even the meanest of us experience at least passing hints of its existence. In these usually all-too-brief moments of heightened calmness and lucidity we see from a perspective that is miraculously free from the petty day-to-day fears and concerns that usually bother us. The higher self needs no one to tell it that it exists. It doesn't need fame, pleasure, sexual gratification, money, power, publishing contracts, elections to public office, or any other mundane prop to feel all right. The higher self feels good by nature because it knows, with an assurance the small self could never even dream of approximating, that it *is*. This knowledge of its true, everlasting, and unshakable existence turns out to be the one thing that the smaller self really wanted all along. It's also the one thing the smaller self will never manage to achieve.

Shutting the Small Self Up

I realize that I already know most of what's necessary to live a meaningful life—that it isn't all that complicated.
—ROBERT FULGHUM, *ALL I REALLY NEEDED TO KNOW
I LEARNED IN KINDERGARTEN*

Shutting the small self up and finding our way back up to that larger and better self for long periods is no easy business, however. Despite the fact that our relationship to the world and everything in it is destined to be plagued with problems unless we learn to act and feel from our higher self, our lower one is always trying to distract us from the task through its never-ending complaints and directives. Indeed, we soon discover that the moment we even slightly decrease the nonstop flow of stimulus, reassurance, and pleasure to it, the lower self produces a racket that makes its normal squawks and squealings mild by comparison. "Feed me!" it yowls. "Stroke me, soothe me, let me know that I exist, that I'm important!"

Such is the din that the lower self creates after only one or two missed feedings that most of us are afraid to stop feeding it at all. However, for those with the fortitude and determination to turn their backs on the lower self for significant periods—for those who, like Emperor Hun Tun, manage to shut off the endless input of the outside world so that nothing enters and nothing distracts—we are told that a fantastic experience awaits. For if it is starved of its normal satisfactions long enough, the wailings of the smaller self eventually die down. When that happens, we can slowly begin to move the seat of our identity up out of the black sludge of selfhood toward that other, larger self, floating quiet and serene far above, like a boat at anchor on a vast blue lake. And when we do that, we stand at least a chance of being genuinely satisfied with our lives for the first time ever.

Perils of the Artist's Path

While all methods of wisdom getting address this journey from lower self to higher (even paths like Buddhism, which deny the self's ultimate existence), the path of the artist has long been one of the most appealing. This is because, from the outside at least, it appears to be easier than any of the others. In fact, on first inspection, getting from small self to large self via the path of creativity seems to offer all the good things that come with this journey without any of the bad. Creativity, after all, is an outpouring from one's deepest being. As such, how could it possibly threaten to take anything of value away from us? In other wisdom paths, where we are asked to deny this or that appetite, to accept this or that teaching, to empty the tepid, uncertain vessel of our private selves into the vast chill ocean of Brahman or the Tao or whatever, it's a different story. The wisdom traditions of the world all proclaim that the ticket necessary to enter the fabulous carnival ride of genuine transcendence is our individual egos—our smaller selves—and that once that ticket is punched, there is no getting it back. Yet with the path of the artist, we appear to have found at last a way out of the miseries of our individual identities and into the higher realms of spirit that allows us to bring at least part of those troublesome but comforting smaller selves of ours along with us for the trip.

This kinder, gentler reputation of the path of creativity is largely an illusion, however, for the smaller self needs to be destroyed just as decisively in the course of it as it does in any other wisdom path. In fact (and as Miller himself suggested here and there in his writing), the process of transcending the smaller self through the creative process might just be the most perilous wisdom-getting method around. For not only does the path of creativity, when genuinely followed, demand just as many sacrifices as other paths do, it also provides a uniquely generous list of pitfalls and snares particular to it. In the vast and anonymous chicken-processing plant of the modern world, where mass-produced sameness is the order of the day and the transcendent is in constant danger of being confused with the merely generic, to actually say good-bye to oneself— even in the service of recovering the larger and truer self that is hiding behind it—always feels, on some level, like the most horrific of mistakes. And this is often particularly the case for those drawn to a creative process. Yet the fact remains that far from being an easy shortcut to enlightenment, the path of the artist is perhaps the most circuitous, treacherous, and potentially disorienting one of all.

Inflating the Smaller Self

The path of the artist is the tough business it is largely because it tends to lead straight *through* the world of the lower, smaller self, rather than away from it. It instructs us to plunge, Arjuna-like, into head-on engagement with the phenomenal universe—the world of the Ten Thousand Things—and to achieve transformation, to die and to be reborn, through directly experiencing all the temptations and confusions that lie in wait there. To be creative is to be caught up in the world, and therefore to be confused, because the world is always busy telling us something other than the straight truth. Thus the more we seem to be succeeding at life and art from the world's perspective, the more we are most likely actually failing.

Fame and praise, should they happen to come along, only intensify these dangers further. "More booze, more mistresses, more adulation!" demands the artist who has surrendered to the siren call of superficial success, all the while refusing to face the fact that he has now forfeited the larger self and the true happiness it could have provided him. Traditional wisdom affirms that the key to being an artist in the deeper and more consequential sense of the word entails avoiding such booby traps by remaining staunchly unmoved by outside opinions, whether they come in the form of praise, scorn, or plain indifference. This emphasis on process rather than product is what Krishna meant in the Bhagavad Gita when he spoke of the action being all and the end nothing. But, as the wisdom traditions also all insist, such perfect equanimity is much easier to theorize about than to actually pull off.

Free to Fail

Every obstacle is an opportunity.
—DR. WAYNE W. DYER, *EVERYDAY WISDOM*

Not that I had to worry too much about any of this as I sat before my empty writing tablet out there on Long Island. Indeed, it was getting clearer to me by the hour that my chances of becoming either a genuine artist or even a bloated faux one were about equally nonexistent. Perhaps, I reasoned, if I had possessed the resolve to continue staring at that page for actual years on end, I might just have succeeded in breaking myself down and building myself up again in the marvelous way that Miller described. But needless to say I didn't have anything like such fortitude, nor did I have anybody around forcing me to even pretend that I did. As usual I was free to do whatever I wanted, and it was slowly starting to occur to me that when it came to getting genuine wisdom, this freedom was the kiss of death.

More and more, as I stared at that grim expanse of empty paper and struggled to push off the moment when I would go down to make lunch or take a walk or answer the phone or do *anything* other than continue to rot within the gray, claustrophobic wastes of my lower self, a new series of thoughts began to cross my mind. There was, I realized, something about my specific position in life at the moment that, good as it looked from the outside, was downright antithetical to the process of getting wise. Fatally infected with a nagging impatience to find out what the experience of enlightenment really felt like—in combination with an absolute inability to suffer the actual work necessary to arrive at that condition—I was drifting further away from my goal with each new scheme I cooked up to get there speedily. While most people who found their way to wisdom seemed to do so either by a transformatory confrontation with life's obstacles or else by a long, steady apprenticeship at some tedious task or other, there simply wasn't anything in my life forcing me to actually undergo either ordeal. And trying to enlighten myself without that added, outside force was like skiing without a mountain or playing tennis with no one on the other side of the net.

Granted, my father really *was* supposed to run out of cash at any minute, and when that finally happened everything in my life would no doubt change radically. But this oft-predicted moment was still in the future. Permissive and generous by nature, my father for the present time always had another couple of hundred bucks for me to avail myself of, and another house to hang out in while I pondered life from a distance for a little while longer. As a result, I was stuck in a wisdom-manual twilight zone, maddeningly free to sample one life option after another, but always moving on to the next before the one I was sampling could do me any real good.

It was clear that I would simply have to find another, more radical way of placing myself in wisdom's path. If I couldn't get wise in college, and I couldn't work my way there Zen-style or create my way there as Henry Miller and people like him had, then I would have to go back to the drawing board and devise a way of making wisdom come to me—of standing in the tracks, as it were, until the wisdom train showed up and just ran me down. With vast relief, I realized it was time to put away the empty writing pad and go in search of a wisdom-getting method that wasn't dependent on my having things like patience or talent or willpower—a way that would change and enlighten me whether I deserved to be so changed and enlightened or not.

THE VISION QUEST

Get Up and Go

While I was eating, a voice came and said: "It is time; now they are calling you." The voice was so loud and clear that I believed it, and I thought I would just go where it wanted me to go.

—BLACK ELK

While some Life Manuals have plots and others don't, the ones that do usually center around a quest. From Jason, Arthur, and the nameless Japanese seeker of the Zen ox-herding series, to the world of *The Celestine Prophecy* and *Mutant Message Down Under,* wisdom books with a story to tell generally tell it about a person who sets out in search of something—a magical plant or elixir, some lost scrolls, or perhaps simply an answer to the question of what life is all about. In traditional cultures, such heroic tales are often closely bound up with actual, highly standardized and ritualized quests that young people are expected to undertake in order to mark their entrance into genuine adulthood. Just as the young members of certain Native American tribes could be accepted as true adults only after they had undergone the trials and insights of the vision quest, so the typical hero or heroine of a quest narrative is not really a complete person before the adventure begins. As the tale opens, it may be just another normal day from the protagonist's perspective. He is bumping along, unaware either that there are any quests to be made or that he is the one to be making them. To be sure, something is missing from his life—but he might not become aware of what that something is until far into the story.

Once the quest commences, this kind of Life Manual often proves to be chockablock full of events in a way that others aren't. Musing and exposition give way to long stretches of straight narrative. Surprises appear, dangers are faced, elaborate hardships are suffered and overcome. By the end of the tale, one can count on the hero being a very different person from the one who started out. If he was a boy when the story began, he is now a man; if he was foolish about the ways of the world, he is now wise to them (thanks at least in part to an encounter with a genuine Adult Unlike Other Adults, who usually appears just when needed to show him the ropes). Perhaps most important, if he was at loose ends in life, never knowing quite what to do with himself or why to do it, he is now the very model of purpose. Knowing the world in a different and deeper way than the run of ordinary mortals, he is ready to cut through life like a plow breaking through soft black earth.

The Journey West

It is natural for man to lead the life of a pilgrim, particularly if that pilgrimage be directed toward a certain goal.

—MICHAEL MAIER

From narrative-centered Life Manuals like *On the Road* to the Castaneda series to *Zen and the Art of Motorcycle Maintenance,* the basics of getting wisdom via travel and adventure were by now clear enough to me. On top of that, I had already taken a shot at such an adventure myself by traveling down to Colombia with Nicky. Of course, that initial attempt had not worked out so well—at least in terms of solid wisdom results. But thanks to my unpleasant weeks at the writing desk I now found myself rethinking just why that might have been. Perhaps, it occurred to me, it wasn't the actual journey aspect that had been a bad idea, but the place I had journeyed to and the things I had done once I got there. In Colombia I had been too wrapped up in trying to follow Nicky's example—too concerned with trying to be a patient, in-the-moment, no-expectations Buddhist. Sure, Nicky was good at that no-expectations stuff, but I wasn't, and it didn't look like I was going to become so either. The time for pursuing enlightenment in coy, roundabout ways was over, and the time for making an unashamedly aggressive bid for the big wisdom payoff was at hand.

America's the Place

As I sat out there on Long Island pondering these new developments, another realization came to me. The country par excellence for this sort of wisdom quest to play itself out in was not some exotic far-off land, but the one I was living in right now. Ironically, America was the place where most of the people who wrote stories about finding themselves actually did the finding. The quintessential stage for the wisdom-hunting drama was right beneath my feet.

The more I thought about it, the more appealing—even downright sensible—a cross-country voyage started to sound. I began to notice that such a journey had been just about mandatory for many of my favorite wisdom authors. Even some of the individuals I didn't directly associate with going off in active search of wisdom had taken time out to travel across America at some point. Both Aldous Huxley and Alan Watts, for example, only commenced their really significant contributions to the Life Manual library after treks by car from the East Coast to California. Seeing as I was now back on the East Coast, at the traditional starting point of such transformational cross-country adventures, why not go on one myself?

The Pattern That Connects

Do you understand that chance encounters often have a deeper meaning?

—JAMES REDFIELD, *THE CELESTINE PROPHECY*

From Bell's theorem, which asserts that one subatomic "object" can affect another such object without even the slightest interval of time or space separating them, to Zen archery, in which archer, arrow, and target are so tied up together that the shot has really been fired before it leaves the bow, wisdom manuals of all stripes bring us the news that everything in life is connected with everything else. Not just connected in a nuts-and-bolts, superficial kind of way, but more deeply and subtly than we can perceive or even imagine. Subject and object, cause and effect, the events of yesterday and of tomorrow: all of these things float in a vast "synchronicitous" soup that we play a part in whether we know it or not.

In Life Manuals featuring a quest, the existence of this deeper pattern of connections tends to be one of the most important discoveries the hero makes along the way. At the start of the tale, the pattern is totally hidden. The hero thinks he lives in a completely mundane universe—one in which a lot of stuff happens, to be sure, but in which it's all more or less random and pointless. As the tale commences and the adventure slowly gets going, however, things change. One after another, coincidences start to occur. People show up at just the right moment and say strangely appropriate things. Events follow one upon another as if an invisible stage director was ordering them to. In fact, it is the events themselves that now start doing the teaching, and the Life Manual author him- or herself often lets those events unfold for long stretches without adding further commentary. The more aware the protagonist becomes of this hidden pattern of connections, the more visible the pattern becomes. Slowly but surely the universe casts off its misleading cloak of ordinariness and shows itself as what it had really been all along: a vast yet intimately interconnected web of pure mystery and magic.

Whatever physical treasures might show up along the way, the real gift to be gained from the quest adventure is the knowledge that just beneath the surface the world really does make sense—and not just any old kind of sense either, but a wild and interesting one at that. As a famous Zen adage has it, every snowflake falls *exactly* where it is supposed to. Having become open to this hidden web of meaning, one understands that life is dull and meaningless only when people choose to *make* it dull and meaningless. Were they to awake, such people would see it all very differently indeed.

Alfonso

Awakening to this larger web of meaning starts with a single event. Someone comes along and tells us something we didn't know just when we need to know it, an opportunity pops up at just the right time, or perhaps a surprise mishap throws our normal life out of gear and introduces us to an unexpected new set of circumstances and possibilities. From there on out, whether we know it or not, the domino chains have started toppling, and we are on our way.

One weekend after several weeks of my creative sequestering, Nicky brought a new guest out to the Long Island house with him—an old friend from his boarding school days named Alfonso. Handsome, refined, and dressed throughout the weekend in a uniform of brightly colored polo shirt, blue jeans, and sockless European loafers, Alfonso had about him the relaxed and gravity-free atmosphere that a lot of Nicky's friends shared. Nicky had mentioned in passing that Alfonso was quite wealthy, and if he hadn't told me so I would have figured it out anyway because he had the money vibe coming off of him in waves. Yet for a wealthy person he also had a number of other, less expected qualities, and over the three-day weekend these gradually came to my notice and stirred my interest more and more. Before I knew it, I had a new subject for my wisdom studies.

Being someone who devoted more than his share of time to questions of life and how to live it—and whose own life at the moment was especially fraught with financial ambiguity—I had given plenty of thought to whether the rich were happier than ordinary folk. As far as I could make out, having lots of money completely solved about 95 percent of life's problems, and because of this, really rich people were indeed enviably relaxed and at ease about 95 percent of the time. However, for the remaining 5 percent or so they often appeared to be even more miserable than the rest of humanity. Behind the playful, tongue-in-cheek, everything's-a-game attitude that this kind of person so often displayed, I could sometimes detect the presence of a vast reservoir of unspeakable boredom and despair— a reservoir that my wisdom manuals were quick to suggest was not a product of my imagination but very real. Appearances aside, being rich, according to the basic Life Manual party line, was nothing to be envied.

The Problem with Money

The main problem with money, of course, was that it fooled those who had it into thinking that they should be happy, when in fact (and as most rich folk found out sooner rather than later) money and happiness weren't really connected at all. Lao-tzu had laid the groundwork for all that the world's wisdom manuals would have to say on the topic with his assertion that the truly rich person was he who had the fewest needs. Thinking initially that they could feed all of their appetites to satiety, most rich people eventually ended up making the discovery that human desire is a hydra-headed monster that grows and multiplies in exact proportion to the degree that it is fed. Satisfy one desire completely, and a whole new bunch will show up to replace it. Likewise with anxiety. No sooner had money laid to rest the run-of-the-mill worries that ordinary working people had to wrestle with than other, more insidious reasons for feeling ill at ease showed up. In every direction, the bright tapestry of wealth was bordered with a black fringe of boredom, angst, and pointlessness. As irritating as it was to have the constant low hum of financial uncertainty in one's life the way I did, and as miserable as it no doubt must have been to have no money at all like the vast majority of the world's population, being loaded was clearly no solution to life's dilemmas either.

A New Solution to an Old Problem

Whether or not they were really as miserable as my Life Manuals told me they were—and as I suspected them to be myself—

most of the handful of rich people I had come into contact with suffered from one indisputably consistent complaint: the world, being theirs for the asking, bored them. Like sticks of asparagus left a little too long in the steamer, these people possessed an essential limpness of spirit—an inability to get really jazzed up about anything that happened to or around them. Some stuff might strike them as funny; some stuff might strike them as pleasurable; some stuff might strike them as amusing (or *divertente,* as the well-heeled Italians in Nicky's circle tended to say); but beyond that, it was by and large very tough to hold these people's interest for too long. Having access to so much pleasure and diversion had robbed them of the power to care about life in a deep and consequential way.

That was why Alfonso was intriguing right off the bat. For loaded though he might have been, there was a distinct quality of enthusiasm at work in him. Rich, young, good-looking, and pleasant to be around, on paper Alfonso was a surefire candidate for spiritual doom. But strangely enough, he didn't seem to be aware of this. Throughout the long weekend, as Nicky and his friends came and went from town and the beach, having picnics on the lawn or tea in the afternoon (while Nicky was off in his room meditating), I watched for some small, telltale sign of essential ennui, some momentary existential flash that would indicate that deep down, Alfonso was as bored as the rest of his ilk.

But none came. Not only was Alfonso's chipper, pleasant attitude consistent through the day and evening hours, but it was accompanied by that unmistakable quality of interest—an easy and amiable attentiveness toward all that was going on around him.

This interest even extended to me. "So what are you up to, Ptolemy?" Alfonso turned and asked me at some point early on in the weekend, with a casualness that suggested we had known each other for years.

"You mean like in general?"

"Well, the next few months for instance. The summer's coming up. What are your plans?"

"I don't have any I guess. I'm kind of just working on my writing right now, but I'm going to have to stop that pretty soon because it's not turning out so well. I'm not really sure what I'm going to do."

"Nicky tells me you're trying to find out what it is you're going to do with your life. I remember being your age, doing that myself. Why don't you think about coming out and staying at the ranch for a while?"

Alfonso's mission control was a large, recently purchased spread in New Mexico just north of Santa Fe—a town whose very name, had I been older and better educated about such things, would have given me my first real hint as to why, though rich, he seemed so happy and at ease all the time. For Alfonso was in fact a member of a very specific breed of wealthy person—one that had emerged in significant numbers with the arrival, in the early seventies, of the New Age. This new breed was both wealthy *and* spiritual, and out to put the lie to the simple equation of money with materialism. If Nicky represented, in some respects at least, the classic model of the child of privilege reacting against that heritage through the aggressive embrace of a nonmaterialistic spiritual path, Alfonso's style of rebellion was of a decidedly different sort. His kind not only had time to spare and money to burn but also a conviction that these blessings need not carry with them a shadow cargo of dissolution and materialistic despair.

Possibility was the buzzword for this new breed. The giddy freedom that came with having scads of cash to spare was now a sensation to be enjoyed, rather than simply a treacherous spiritual trap to be avoided. For in fact, the universe really *was* full of unlimited possibility. So why shouldn't access to money make that truth more apparent, at least under the right conditions? Once again taking the clue from Lao-tzu (though this time to make a very different point), the wealthy-but-spiritual person counseled acceptance of one's circumstances—even if those circumstances happened to be incredibly fortunate. Rather than suffer guilt for their unusual freedoms, rich New Agers could feel called upon to simply make the most of them. You could relax, have a great time in life . . . *and* be spiritual at the same time! In fact, in this new amalgamation of values, the degree to which one was relaxed and not hung up about one's money was precisely an indication of just how advanced, spiritually speaking, a person was.

In recent years, people more or less like Alfonso had been buying up great chunks of land in spots like Sedona, Arizona, and Crestone, Colorado (and Santa Fe, New Mexico), and like Alfonso they often did so without knowing exactly what they would do with this land once they had it. Like others of his breed, Alfonso had fallen in love with the bright, elemental openness of the Southwest, and was operating on the assumption that the knowledge of just what to do with his property would show up in the future, when it needed to. In the meantime, there was no particular hurry about anything. Things would gel when they were ready to, and there was nothing wrong with having fun while waiting for this to happen.

A Place in the Desert

Though I might not have understood all the sociocultural permutations of Alfonso's rich-but-spiritual lifestyle, it seemed that he really meant what he said about me coming to stay at his ranch. Out of the blue, I had been presented with the perfect host for a potential cross-country journey—a strong, single tack upon which to hang my entire adventure.

"You mean I could come and just hang out for a couple of days? I've always wanted to see the desert."

"Hang out for a couple of weeks if you want! There's plenty of room, and I love to have company."

The weekend was gone before I knew it and so were Nicky and his friends—including Alfonso. But suddenly the empty house and writing pad, and the indeterminacy of my plans for the future, didn't bother me in the least. Like a supersaturated solution just waiting to receive the pinprick that will turn it into a solid, my vague and wishy-washy summer plans had suddenly cohered. I would head west and come back different. One way or another, Big Changes would occur in the course of my adventure, and thanks to them I would return to my old world with the tools I needed to climb out of the weird, parenthetical limbo I was stuck in and really get on with things. Thanks to the knowledge I would gain out on the road, I would be able to put my life into gear at last.

Preparations

Deep summer seemed like the right time for such a journey, and as it was only late spring now, I would be idling on the East Coast for a while more. That was no problem though, because now I had a goal—a main course around which to arrange the formerly shapeless garnish of my days. Before too long my father and stepmother showed up on Long Island and I wasn't by myself five days a week anymore. Elena came out to visit a couple of times as well, and I had the opportunity to further compare my life to hers. As usual, the whole cross-country idea didn't make too much sense to her, but by now I was comfortable with the fact that she simply didn't have my perspective on life and so shouldn't ever be expected to understand what I was up to. In June I went down to McLean to spend some time with my mother, and as soon as I got there friends of my parents hired me for a monthlong job helping with their house renovation in Georgetown. The work gave further shape to the days, and the indeterminacy of my life beyond the summer (for I was now out of college officially and had nowhere special to be the coming fall) was entirely tolerable too. My journey west, I was now quite certain, would take care of everything.

As the days passed and I worked at the Georgetown job, the specifics of my journey began to take shape. The first issue was transportation. Life Manual purist that I was, hitchhiking was of course high on the list of options, but this was vetoed almost immediately by my normally agreeable mother, who also put the kibosh on my second inspiration—a motorcycle. The solution eventually arrived at was for my mother to lend me her recently purchased '79 Pontiac Sunbird. With its white exterior and bright red upholstery, it was clearly a little garish for my purposes, and I puzzled over whether someone should really undertake a life-changing cross-country journey in such a car. However, it was nice of my mother to offer it, and even though a battered jalopy would have been more appropriate, I realized that I didn't much want to break down out there on the open road. So the Sunbird it was to be.

The weeks passed. Elena came to visit one more time before going off to Italy for some summer courses in Art History, and before I knew it July arrived and my journey was set to commence. I now had some cash saved up from my Georgetown job, but my father gave me an American Express card to use as I needed as well. Just what might constitute "needed" was, of course, a little unclear, and the card became yet another symbol of the confused and contradictory financial situation I was stuck in. According to the most recently overheard reports, the family financial boat was continuing to sink, and sooner rather than later I would be forced to jump into the chill waters of Real Life and swim for it. When this finally happened, there was no question that I would be far better off if I had already succeeded in getting enlightened—and my cross-country journey was my last and most clear-cut shot at making this happen. I pocketed the credit card and hoped for the best.

Busting Open My Psyche

The soul must needs go through a season of trial, and were it suddenly plunged into a state of rest, it would not know how to use it.

—FRANÇOIS FÉNELON

Another key preparatory aspect of the trip—in fact, the most important one—was how to be certain that once out on the road I really would have the super-significant, life-changing experience that I was banking on. One thing was for sure: I was not about to set myself up for another anticlimax. There would be no more drunken shamans, no more half-baked, inconclusive adventures, no more empty writing pads. One way or another, this time around something was going to *happen*, and I needed to take all measures necessary to ensure that it did.

But what were these measures to be? There was no question that the nameless Something that was to occur out there on the open highway would involve wrestling the smaller self out of the driver's seat—delivering it a sufficiently stunning blow so that the larger self would finally be able to move over and take the wheel. Like a child who, after trying and trying to tease open a puzzle, just gives up and smashes it on the floor, I was getting more and more intrigued with the notion of simply *assaulting*

my smaller self in some manner. I was also starting to appreciate, more than ever before, that this experience might not be
an especially pleasant one to undergo.

I had plenty of material to back me up in this suspicion.
After all, rough and wrenching transformational experiences
abounded in certain of my Life Manuals—especially in those
centered around quests of one sort or another. In *Zen and the Art
of Motorcycle Maintenance*, Robert Pirsig had actually gone crazy
and received shock treatment in the course of coming to
understand what life was all about. And Castaneda, in his
books, provided me with endless examples of this kind of trans-
formation-through-trauma. Following don Juan about through
the sands of the Sonora, the unwitting Carlos was constantly
being paralyzed with fear, feeling his stomach seize up with
terror, all but losing control of his bowels, and otherwise getting shaken up by the more-than-human powers waiting for
him out there. In *Tales of Power*, he had actually leapt off the face
of a cliff and felt his personality disintegrating like a broken
necklace of brightly colored beads. In Castaneda's world, there
was no question that psychic transformation could sting.

Yet it was also the case that in the long run this didn't really
matter. If genuine change usually didn't feel all that good while
it was happening, it still eventually turned out to be for the
best. For all that Carlos got jerked and jangled and bugged out
by his crazy desert adventures, the discomforts he experienced
came along with fantastic psycho-spiritual changes that made
it all worthwhile. By getting scared out of his wits, Carlos was
always being knocked a few rungs further up the ladder of
knowledge. With a payoff like that, who could complain?

The Food of the Gods

Early on in his adventures, Carlos had learned that hallucinogenic drugs were an invaluable tool in the sort of education-through-terror that don Juan was making him undergo. While not a key aspect of the sorcerer's path, the right drugs could work like metaphysical Drano, clearing out psychic pipes that years of inculcation in the Western rational mind-set had hopelessly clogged.

It was getting fairly obvious that this kind of radical, no-nonsense, psychic drain cleaning was just what I was in need of myself. It was time to stop fooling around—time to give my Westernized, consensus-bound consciousness a real run for its money. If so far I had been drifting here and there on the great and wide river of wisdom, the time had come to swim straight for the falls. Once out on the road I would track down the right kind of hallucinogenic drugs, take a whole bunch of them, and get my psyche revamped in the sort of turbulent but decisive fashion that Castaneda had experienced. The shit would hit the fan, my smaller self would be blown to pieces, my larger self would seize control, and I—definitively and decisively wiser for the experience—would be able to get on with my life at last.

The Sorcerer's Apprentice

Up to this point, drugs had played a surprisingly small part in my life. Never a fan of marijuana, I had by and large avoided heavier drugs too, even after people like Watts and Huxley started dropping unsubtle hints that these substances were just the ticket for those unable to manage the breakthrough into wisdom by other means. Before leaving Vassar, I had had my first brush with a powerful hallucinogen in the company of a couple of friends, including the girl with the *I Ching* skills, out on the campus golf course. I was handed a little square of paper with a picture of Mickey Mouse dressed up in his Sorcerer's Apprentice garb from *Fantasia* on it, and told to chew it slowly.

I had nothing against Mickey Mouse, but this incidental packaging detail struck me as a telling indication that a factory-made, synthetic substance like LSD was not going to give me the sort of whole-cloth wisdom encounter I was really looking for. There seemed to me to be something a little gauche in seeking as elusive and mysterious a thing as wisdom in a substance of any kind—much less one that came with a Disney cartoon stamped on it.

My initial suspicions had turned out to be correct. Once chewed and swallowed, the little Mickey Mouse tab had delivered four hours or so of fun-house mental warping and the sort of passing, momentarily profound insights that I was familiar with from my marginal marijuana smoking over the course of my high school years. It was all interesting enough, but for someone as saturated with the wisdom canon as I was it was certainly not the definitive transformational adventure I was hoping for. When Mickey's effects wore off I felt much the same as I had been before, only with a slightly hindered ability to concentrate on my Life Manuals that lasted for a couple of days. If I could get there otherwise, I had decided at that point, my particular road to the palace of wisdom would not involve hallucinogenic substances. I would leave such quick-fix solutions to others.

Time for a Shortcut

That was then, however, and some seven months later I was having very definite second thoughts about the matter. If drugs were the royal road to wisdom for those who didn't have luck with other methods, then it was clear that I was fast qualifying as a good candidate for them.

However, I was still not going to settle for a drug that came with Mickey Mouse's picture on it. What I needed was something more exotic: something along the lines of the organic, hard-to-find substances that Castaneda described so appealingly in his books. If I was going to take the substance route after all, I would see to it that I did so with jimsonweed, datura, morning glory seeds, peyote buttons, or perhaps those elusive powdered mushrooms that Castaneda mentioned so frequently. Rereading a few pages of *The Doors of Perception*, I reacquainted myself with the mystique of that glass of mescaline-laced water Huxley had downed, and of how, thanks to it, he had discovered that the hedge at the bottom of the garden was really the Buddha-nature itself. If substance-fueled wisdom had been good enough for Huxley, I realized, there really was no reason why I shouldn't put my disappointing experience with Mickey Mouse behind me and try it myself. I would find some suitably rustic, straight-out-of-the-ground substance, and I would take it in suitably romantic and portentous conditions. And I would take a whole lot of it. When I did, wisdom would simply have nowhere left to hide.

Hitting the Road

So it was that on a bright July morning I threw a few bags in the back of the Sunbird, gave my mother a hug good-bye, and pulled onto the broad, black, fast-moving lanes of Route 495 South.

When you're on a Kerouacian odyssey you're supposed to take the blue highways—the ones that meander past flashing streams and under leafy, Whitmanesque oaks spreading their generous branches to the four directions. You're supposed to stop and share friendly scraps of talk with local people you've never seen before but somehow feel like you've known all your life. The code of the cross-country quest dictates that you

enter America in a completely relaxed and informal manner—
as if the whole country were no more than a vast green park
you happened to stroll into on a Sunday afternoon. Thanks to
your having made yourself available to the magic of chance,
life somehow opens up and intensifies. Wild, unlikely encounters and events transpire. Stories are made.

At least that's the way it's supposed to work. Days one, two,
and three of my adventure came and went, however, without
my enjoying so much as one Kerouacian encounter. Not a single weirdly spontaneous interaction with any wise, white-
bearded wheat farmers, misty-eyed hoboes, or raven-haired
diner waitresses had taken place, and I was starting to suspect
that they were not going to either. Mile after mile of America
clicked by, with no visible indication of when I should pull off
the main highway and plunge into the weaving macadam back-
roads that would lead me, curve by unexpected curve, to the
verdant, mystical bosom of America. Before I knew it the floor
of the car was littered with gas station receipts and fast food
wrappers, and I had spent three comfortable but indistinguish-
able nights in motels watching a series of distinctly non-
Kerouacian television sets while waiting for the coffee I had drunk
in the course of the day to wear off so that I could fall asleep.
By day three I had put over a thousand miles between me and
northern Virginia, but my trip had really yet to begin. I also
knew that if I wasn't careful, it might not do so at all.

American Express

For this fact I could not really blame America itself, however.
The visionary zeitgeist may have been at a low ebb during that
summer of 1981, but the real problem lay with me, and I knew
it. To begin with, I was entirely too well prepared for my journey. The Sunbird was in excellent condition and not about to

break down. The American Express card in my pocket made interaction with fellow seekers of food and shelter an unlikelihood, as all I needed to secure a roof over my head each night was to pull off the highway at practically any exit and extend this card at a motel reception desk. Shy by nature, I needed the goad of necessity to ensure interaction with others, and as usual all such goads were absent. With American Express on board, the forces of serendipitous mystery seemed to be keeping their distance.

No doubt all this would change by the time I got to New Mexico, but it was a shame that I was covering the miles in between with such swift and unvisionary efficiency. If a key part of being on a quest was heeding the right incidental detail, of turning off the road at just the appropriate exit and striking up a conversation with just the predestined person, I had to admit that I didn't feel especially gifted in this department. The domino chains of didactic coincidence were no doubt out there somewhere, waiting to start toppling, but behind the wheel on Interstate 40, rushing along with all the other cars through the Carolinas and Tennessee and Arkansas, it was hard for me to know just where that first domino lay waiting to be tipped.

All Those Years Ago

Late on day three I crossed into Oklahoma and spent the night at another Motel 6—a chain that had become my stop of preference. Apparently Motel 6 had originally taken its name from the six dollars it charged for a room when it first opened for business. That summer, a single room cost $16.95 plus tax. When, I wondered, had one of these rooms actually cost six dollars? Like just about every other aspect of my trip, the question conjured up images of a time now past—a time when life was simpler, cheaper, and easier to negotiate. On the radio that first summer after John Lennon's assassination, "All Those Years Ago," George Harrison's tribute to him, repeated endlessly. The song fairly dripped with unapologetic nostalgia for a vanished time of freedom and possibility, and as I listened to it out on that big bland highway every twenty-five minutes or so, it certainly seemed like George might have had a point.

Day four of my journey dawned as bright and cryptic as the three that had come before. I packed up my bags with their loose assemblage of clothing, toiletries, and Life Manuals and got back onto the straight strip of Interstate 40 heading for the Texas Panhandle. Somewhere along this stretch, as morning gave way to afternoon and the car hummed on without so much as the smallest Kerouacian cough or rattle, the country around me seemed to relax and open up a little; and as it did so, I did too. As I crossed over into Texas, the wind roared through the open windows with a new kind of warmth and texture. I was still stuck in my smoothly running cage of a car, still tracing a hopelessly straight and solitary line across the country, but I *was* getting farther and farther from where I had come. Here in this rich red landscape, where even the crows perched on the passing billboards looked bigger, blacker, and more consequential than their eastern cousins, the simple fact that I was somewhere else started to count for something.

The Tao of Cigarettes

With windows down and the all-but-empty car a roaring cockpit of wind, I moved up the fresh black strip of road through cool lakes of cloud-created darkness that alternated with long, warm stretches of light. Bulky white clouds moved in procession through the sky above, and I could see the edges of the shadows of these clouds as they made their way across the great chessboard of sand and chaparral on either side of me.

That *was* chaparral out there, wasn't it? I didn't really know what the stuff was supposed to look like, but Carlos and don Juan were always running through it on their various metaphysical desert errands, so it seemed logical that it would be growing in a place like this.

Before I knew it Texas was behind me and I was actually in New Mexico. The closer each green highway sign told me I was to Santa Fe, the more intensely did I feel the truth of that mantra endlessly uttered by so many of my tutelary voices: things are different out west. The big travel-or-stay-home dilemma I had been wrestling with back east now had its answer. The ancient Taoists, with all their injunctions to stay put rather than seek enlightenment elsewhere, obviously had never seen a place like McLean, Virginia. Surely if they had, they would have told me to hotfoot it out of there as soon as possible and seek satisfaction with the moment only when I had managed to find a place like this.

One of the tools for passing the time that I had been making use of during the drive were cigarettes. By the time we left Colombia I had become something of a fan of Fernando's Pielrojas myself, and once back in the States and stationed at my writing desk, I had discovered how truly invaluable these items were in the battle against mundane time—the endless, noncommittal minutes that made up ordinary adult life. Every few miles I would reach for a Marlboro, and the windy interior of the car would swirl with bits of ash like the buzzing heart of one of those atoms I had read about in *The Tao of Physics* and *The Dancing Wu Li Masters*.

I took the exit Alfonso had indicated and headed north on a smaller four-lane road that eventually passed through what looked like the outskirts of Santa Fe proper. Low, adobe-style buildings had been increasing in frequency along the highway and now they were everywhere. Those *were* adobe-style buildings, weren't they? As usual, I knew the term only from reading. But these round-edged, sand-colored structures seemed to fit the word, just as the vegetation of the harsh but pleasant desert answered to my expectations of what chaparral would be. Whatever the proper names for all of this stuff were, it was clear that I had found my way into a landscape similar to the cactus-studded wonderlands that graced the covers of books like *Journey to Ixtlan* and *Tales of Power*. If my great ambition had long been to find myself actually inside one of those books instead of stuck out beyond them, it was easy to feel that I was closer to that condition now than I had ever been before.

I pulled into the parking lot of a mini-mall with a convenience store and a Laundromat and stretched my legs while a tall, sullen-looking man with a striking, Indian-looking profile finished speaking on the single pay phone. I dialed Alfonso's number.

I had not spoken to Alfonso for over two weeks, and was half expecting him to be surprised, and perhaps displeased, to learn that I was now just around the corner. "Oh, it's you," I imagined him saying, suddenly cold to the prospect of a new hanger-on arriving at his ranch without any solid sort of reason for being there. "What do you want?"

My fears were in vain. Over the line, Alfonso's voice transmitted that same sense of ease and comfort it had back on Long Island. He spoke to me as if we had known each other all our lives and it had only been a day or so since we last had talked. He gave me some simple instructions, and ten minutes later I was turning the Sunbird down a driveway stretching straight for a quarter mile or so through the slowly darkening desert. The house was visible from a long way off, but the closer I got the more it eluded comprehension. It seemed to be made up of roundish, sand-colored blocks, like a child's fort. Rather than beginning or ending anywhere in particular, it rose up and died away in a series of noncommittal humps and curves. I presumed it was adobe.

More Lessons on Doing-Not-Doing

"You're downstairs in my old meditation room. It's small but it's got a good vibe."

After greeting me warmly and showing me around inside and out, Alfonso—still in one of those crisp polo shirts—left me to my own devices in my new quarters: a small, nondescript room with whitewashed walls, a bed and bedside table with a lamp, and not much else. The space had a monkish spareness that I found appealing. On the far side of the room, a pair of tall glass doors faced south onto the desert.

After a shower, I dressed and made my way upstairs into the main living space—not that there was much evidence of living going on. The house's interior was just as confusing as its exterior, with stairs and hallways running off in all directions. Sparse Southwestern-style furniture stood here and there, none of it looking very lived-in. Up a short stairway, in an area directly over my bedroom, was a long, high-ceilinged room that from where I stood didn't seem to have anything in it at all. I walked up and stuck my head all the way in. Nothing. It was entirely empty, all the way down to the rugless, red tile floor. On the east and west walls, high windows opened onto an empty, darkening sky.

I stepped back down the steps and entered the kitchen. Though rustic, it was permeated with the same feeling of relaxed opulence as the rest of the house. It was Southwestern opulence—made of rough surfaces and earth tones—but once one got used to reading it correctly, it telegraphed the existence of large amounts of cash as clearly as any tennis court or sailboat did back east.

Alfonso appeared again now, a sweater around his shoulders and his sandy hair brushed back from his high, broad forehead. He flashed me a grin and gave me a whack on the shoulder.

"*Quieres ir a comer, amigo?*"

"What's that?" Despite all my days down in Colombia, I still didn't understand much Spanish.

"*Comer!* Want to get something to eat?"

"Oh! Sure."

Throughout dinner at a restaurant in downtown Santa Fe, Alfonso spoke with his usual cheerful enthusiasm, moving from one topic to another, never quite monopolizing the conversation but always stopping to draw me in as well. Alfonso had been to a great many places and done a great many things in his short and privileged life, and now, he told me, all he really wanted to do was hang out here in the desert.

"So what do you do while you hang out?"

"*Doing,*" said Alfonso. "It's such a serious word, isn't it? *Do* this, *do* that. I got so much of all that when I was a kid—at boarding school, then later in college too, when I was your age. Now I guess you could say my real interest is in *being.*"

The more we talked, the more the differences in Nicky's and Alfonso's solutions to the conundrums presented by ordinary life became clear. If Nicky had outfitted himself with pads and helmet for a really serious charge down the spiritual ball field, Alfonso was more of a Sunday afternoon player. There was no tackling allowed in his game book, and apparently not much in the way of definite goals to run toward either. After dinner we got back in Alfonso's blue Mercedes and drove around for a while—without any particular destination but just to get some more of the atmosphere of the place. Up above us a partial moon hung in the blue-black sky, casting considerable illumination down on the landscape for all its slimness. Lit by this sliver of moon, the clouds continued to move and change as they had in the full blaze of the day, giving the impression that I had arrived at a sort of windswept, cosmic nerve center—a place where things were always coming and going, where something was always happening.

The Tao of Cigarettes, Continued

At a certain point Alfonso turned into a convenience store. I followed him in and looked around, but I had been through so many of these in the last several days that none of the items looked appealing. Alfonso being the sophisticated, dust-repelling millionaire he was, I felt a little awkward being in the store with him at all. With its hunting magazines, overbright lights, and rotating hot dogs, it was far more a part of my world than his, and I instinctively felt like I should be whisking him back out of it.

This awkward feeling lessened abruptly as I watched Alfonso walk over to the Indian girl behind the counter and request a pack of Camels.

"Nonfilters, huh?" I said when we were in the Mercedes again as Alfonso punched in the lighter. "I didn't know you smoked."

Alfonso flashed his toothy smile. "I don't!" he said brightly. "That is, I don't smoke in the way that someone does who's on some identity trip about it. You know, like: 'Yes, yes, I smoke. I've got to quit.' Or 'Yes, yes, I smoke, I don't care about my body or myself.' To me"— and here Alfonso held up the freshly opened pack, as if he were delivering an educational lecture on it—"this is just a pack of cigarettes. Nothing less, nothing more. It doesn't stand for some heavy kind of thing I need to wrestle with. It isn't something that controls what or who I am. It's something I can pick up and interact with if I choose to, but which I can just as easily put down and forget about. I can see

through these guys. I know they can demand this huge investment of head space, but it's an investment I don't choose to
make."

Alfonso took a drag and blew a stream of blue smoke out the
half-open window as he pulled the Mercedes back out onto the
road. "And what's so wild, Ptolemy, is that once you say No to
all of that—once you decline the invitation to get involved
with an identity issue about whether you do or you don't want
to smoke, and all the junk that goes along with it, everything
changes. The cigarettes become what they really are, which is
nothing. They may be part of the trip today, right now . . . but
that doesn't mean they will be tomorrow. Tomorrow's just an
abstraction anyway! So right now, just this second—this timeless moment that's really the same thing as the big Now that's
always happening—I think I'll have a smoke."

Listening to Alfonso go on, I started to feel like a cigarette
myself. I bummed one from him and accepted a light as we
sped away, back toward the ranch.

The Days That Followed

#174: Encourage your children to have a part-time job after
the age of sixteen.

—*LIFE'S LITTLE INSTRUCTION BOOK*

Over the next week or so, Alfonso and I spent a lot of time in
that blue Mercedes. I soon became very comfortable in
Alfonso's company and learned to take his generosity in stride
without feeling too embarrassed by it. There was a lot of daylight in Santa Fe in the middle of the summer, and without anything in the way of work, the two of us were called upon to
come up with endless projects to pass the time. Most of these
had run-of-the-mill focuses like food or sightseeing or running

small errands for the ranch, and as we went about them Alfonso would expand upon the issue of smoking or not smoking, or what life out here in Santa Fe (or "Fanta Se," as he liked to call it) meant to him, and any number of other topics.

There were a handful of others living on the ranch—men and women, all of them somewhere in their late twenties or early thirties, mostly friends of Alfonso's who just seemed to have ended up there. To varying degrees these people played a part in our activities as well, but by and large their schedules didn't overlap with Alfonso's and mine. Other than Zack, a friendly, bearded fellow who seemed to function as a general caretaker, I was never really clear about what any of them were doing at the ranch. They were all pleasant enough, however, and it seemed to be understood by everyone that I was the special guest of the moment, and that it was natural that Alfonso should be going out of his way to make sure that I had a good time.

Alfonso was a master of navigating the great empty spots in the day, swinging from moment to moment with the aid of the ever-ready Mercedes and the Camel pack, which sat between us as we drove about and which, thanks to Alfonso's encouraging rhetoric, I could help myself to without any left-brain concerns about getting "hooked" on them. We visited restaurant after restaurant, and Alfonso kept paying for the food. We drove up to Taos and elsewhere in the surrounding desert country, looking at the native buildings, passing through mile after mile of red-sand scenery and fathomless cobalt sky.

And before a week was up, I found myself getting restless. There was, I had started to realize, something about blazingly hot places that just seemed to raise with special vigor the question of what to do with oneself. Despite the beauty of the landscape, and Alfonso's skills as a tour guide, I couldn't help but start to feel that there was a certain inconclusiveness to our adventures. After all, I was on a transformational quest—and all the stuff we did, while pleasant and diverting, wasn't really furthering me in the tasks that I had set for myself. What was everybody really *up* to out here, under the measureless dome of the Southwestern sky? How did people end up in the places they did in life? What was the real point of any of it?

In spite of these reservations on my part, and even though I detected hints of a certain ennui and lack of purpose going on with some of the others at the ranch as well, Alfonso himself continued to give the impression that he didn't suffer from any such problems. "Who knows what this place is going to become in time, Ptolemy?" he would remark. "I know *I* don't. But I do know that if I create a space in which something extraordinary can happen, then extraordinary stuff will be a whole lot more likely to show up than if I didn't."

In addition to Alfonso and his friends, there was another group of people out at the ranch who did not appear to be suffering from any confusions about how to pass the day. These were the local Hispanic and Indian laborers who showed up each morning, hours before I stumbled out of the meditation room, and set to work in the area behind the main house putting up the buildings in which Alfonso's extraordinary stuff was to someday take place. Short, dark, and uniformly muscular, these intense, cheerful men toiled away under the blazing New Mexico sun deep into the afternoon, with an energy so tireless it made me dizzy just to contemplate. Squinting out at them from the protective shadows of the house, I would be overcome afresh with disappointment at how I was going about my life. One more time, all the familiar questions about how best to spend one's days made their way through my head, leaving me as stumped as ever. Was the choice really between joining the ranks of the financially unblessed, doing actual, no-fooling work for hours on end like those distant laborers, or simply tooling about in a Mercedes smoking cigarettes to which I wasn't attached, like Alfonso? The insufficiency of these two choices was painfully exacerbated by the realization that my own imminent future didn't allow me to take choice number two even if I wanted to. Try as I might at moments to pretend otherwise, it was still painfully obvious that I was as far as I ever was from fitting myself into the adult landscape.

Just at the point when these realizations really started to bear down upon me, Alfonso would always breeze in and whisk me off in the Mercedes—to pick up some vegetables or look at some furniture or do some other pleasant errand that would make the weight of the moment go away. And so it went for day after day. Out in the blasting summer heat the laborers labored, and inside, beneath the shade of the house or in the air-conditioned coolness of the Mercedes or yet another restaurant, Alfonso and I would hang out and bide our time between transparent Camel nonfilters, letting the conversation go where it would.

Powerful Stuff

"So, Alfonso, do you have any idea where I could get some peyote buttons?"

The question came one day as the two of us were making our way into town for another late breakfast.

"Peyote buttons?" Alfonso sounded surprised.

"Yeah. Don't they grow out here?"

"I guess so, but I've never run into any."

"Oh."

Alfonso could tell I was disappointed by his answer, and as usual he set himself to putting the situation right.

"There's plenty of mushrooms around, though."

"Like hallucinogenic mushrooms you mean?"

"Mm-hmm. They're not really my bag anymore, but I've had some great experiences with them out here."

"Do you think you could get me some?"

Alfonso thought for a moment. "Sure. I don't see why not. Very powerful stuff. You've never tried them?"

"No."

"Well, this is definitely the place to do it. I'll have to make some calls."

"They're not expensive, are they?"

"Oh, don't worry about that. Remember—you're my guest."

Though the least exotic-sounding item on the list of approved visionary substances I had put together, mushrooms had been mentioned in a sufficient enough number of my Life Manuals for me to be delighted with Alfonso's response. "Powerful stuff" was just what I had been hoping for, and I found myself wondering why it had taken me so long to bring up the topic.

That evening Alfonso made a couple of calls and reported that it would take two or three days for the mushrooms to show up. However, they would be of very high quality once they did arrive. There was also a fortuitous aspect to the delay, as Alfonso explained to me the next day over breakfast.

"You know, Ptolemy, I was thinking about this last night. I don't think I'm going to take any mushrooms myself this time around, so I see myself as your guide on this adventure. What I'd like to do is make absolutely sure that you have the best trip possible. My friend isn't going to get the mushrooms till at least Thursday, and this weekend's the full moon. So it seems to me that you're being given a gift here. A hallucinogen is only a meaningful experience if you allow it to be, and I think you have an opportunity to create an experience that really *is* meaningful. But we've got to do some work first."

If for no other reason, this disclosure from Alfonso was interesting for the fact that it included the word *work*. Out of the blue, it looked like the two of us had been given a genuine project—something that we could really throw ourselves into. But the details were still unclear. What, exactly, did Alfonso mean by work?

"The thing about heavy hallucinogens," Alfonso explained, "is that they can only interact with the material you give them. You want this to be a really significant experience, right? Not just some trippy good-time thing."

"Oh yeah," I said, excited that Alfonso understood what I was looking to get without my having to explain it to him. "I want this to be *important*."

"Good. The first thing we need to do then is clean you up."

"Clean me up?"

"Yup. The fewer impurities you have in your system, the better. We've got to create both a physical and a psychological space for the mushrooms to work in—one where you can actually receive what they have to teach you. That means cleaning and refining your system—really getting it set up for the experience. Now it turns out that the mountain behind the house is a perfect location for an intense mushroom experience. It's been known for hundreds, maybe thousands of years as a heavy spot—a place where energies gather. The Indians who used to live here used it as a center of pilgrimage. We're going to take advantage of that. We're also going to take advantage of the time of the month. We're going to take advantage of everything. A full moon in three days! It's perfect for what I've got in mind."

There was no question about it—the dominoes had started to fall. It was also quite obvious that in coming up with this project, I had done Alfonso a favor just as he was doing me one.

That night, under a moon slightly but noticeably fuller than the day before, we drove into town for my last meal. I ate a fair bit, and fell asleep full of happy apprehension.

Cleaning House

From your boyhood you would have studied and prepared yourself to pass the test—to live alone for four days and nights without water or food on the sacred mountain. A respected older man, perhaps an uncle, would be your "sponsor" and teacher, helping you to prepare. Finally the long anticipated day would come. You would say goodbye to your mother and father, knowing that when you returned from the mountain you would never live as a child in their lodge.

—STEVEN FOSTER AND MEREDITH LITTLE, DESCRIBING THE TRADI-
TIONAL CHEYENNE RITES OF PASSAGE FOR YOUNG MEN

The following morning I got out of bed early, and watched the sun rise and the laborers collect around the half-constructed buildings. Without food to go in search of, I imagined that there would be less to fill the day with—but in thinking this I was underestimating Alfonso. When he appeared later in the morning, it was clear that he was now even more energized by the structure and purpose that the Mushroom Project had provided than he had been the day before.

"So what's up for today?" I asked as he ate his breakfast and I sipped at a cup of hot water with lemon he had prepared for me.

"It's off to the baths, my man. The cleansing has officially begun."

"Baths?"

"Half an hour north of here. Very curative waters. It's a perfect spot to sweat the impurities out of your system. From here on out you're going to drink lots and lots of water, but that's it.

Nothing else is going to go into your system. That way, when you take those mushrooms your body will be in as pure and prepared a state as possible. It's the perfect first step."

"How about cigarettes?"

"Oh, they're okay. Tobacco was used by the Indians in their sweat lodges. It's a purificant."

Alfonso's baths were located in a squat, square cement building lying just off a winding mountain road that we hadn't yet traveled on our afternoon drives. Walking through the low entrance door, a sulfury smell and a warm cloud of steam overwhelmed me. When my eyes had adjusted to the light, I saw a large room taken up by an ancient, shallow swimming pool. From one side to another, a collection of whiskered men, most of them in their fifties or beyond, stared up at us like walruses regarding an Arctic explorer. Looking at these men as they paddled and puffed about in this curious grotto stuck incongruously out there in the desert, I had the unmistakable sense that, for better or worse, my transformatory journey had at last begun in earnest.

Alfonso led me to the changing area, where, following his example, I left my clothes, watch, and wallet in a clammy, rust-mottled locker. Once in the water I floated dutifully about and felt my body relax a little under the heat. Somewhere, a filter gurgled softly. Alfonso seemed to know some of the other men in the water with us, and as he chatted with them, I tried to get a handle on my mood. Lunchtime had arrived, but I found that the hunger that had been growing in an irritating way throughout the morning had fallen away, to be replaced by a light-headedness that, like the greenish water, was at once unnerving and strangely pleasant.

"So you think this is really going to make a difference when I take the mushrooms, huh?" I asked Alfonso as we bobbed about.

"Oh, absolutely. What you want in a situation like this is to create a pure space within you—physically *and* spiritually—where the mushrooms can work. We spend so much of our time filling ourselves up with stuff—with ideas, with actions, with pleasure, with opinions about things—but when we approach these powerful plants, we need to be empty: just like the big room back at the ranch is empty. That room is far and away the most powerful space on the property. And you know why? Simply because there's nothing in it. People are the same way. By coming at the mushrooms and the power they hold with nothing inside you but willingness, you make it possible for them to really do a number on you."

By the time Alfonso and I had logged an hour or so in the pool and retired for a mud bath, a mood of such intense expectancy had taken over that I wasn't even bothered by the slight headache I had developed. Driving home in the Mercedes with an evening and a full day of fasting still to come, I reveled in the feeling of no longer being just a bumble-headed teenager but a full-fledged Man with a Purpose. For the first time since I had read about it over a year before, I was to be investigating the visionary landscape firsthand. If the Buddha was the hedge at the bottom of the garden, if Mescalito was waiting to appear among the cacti, and if I really was the world and the world really was me, I was now to *know* these things, rather than only knowing *about* them courtesy of my Life Manuals.

The next morning Alfonso went off to see his mysterious friend, and when he returned an hour later with the goods, I was a little taken aback at how completely benign they looked. Emptied out onto the kitchen table from the little leather sack they came in, the mushrooms resembled, to my eyes, the dried remains of some tiny chopped-up sea creature.

"Don't let their looks fool you," said Alfonso. "These beauties are supercharged. My man guarantees it."

"So what do I do?" I said, still examining the twisted, mummified curiosities one by one. "Eat all of them?"

"Well, I've been thinking about that. There's really just about enough for two people here. Taking half of them would get you off pretty well, but this is one of those once-in-a-lifetime opportunities. We know that you're serious about having an experience you'll remember, and we know that it would be a shame to compromise that seriousness by not taking enough. I think you might as well eat the whole bag."

Good News and Bad News

Then you would go with the medicine chief to the sacred mountain, where you would be given a buffalo robe to wrap around you if it got cold. The medicine chief would leave you there and you would remain for four days and nights, facing your childhood fears, your loneliness and boredom, your hunger and thirst, seeking a vision for yourself and for the people of your community. When your quest ended, you would return to the medicine chief who would take you to the council of elders. There you would tell the story of your vision quest and the meaning of your experience would be interpreted by the wise ones. You would receive a new name, a "medicine name," based on your vision quest. Your own private symbols or insignia would also be revealed to you. Afterward, you would not live at home. Henceforth you hunted and rode with the men and became eligible for marriage.

—STEVEN FOSTER AND MEREDITH LITTLE

By the morning of day three, the hunger that had nagged at me on and off the previous two days had largely vanished. My concentration, which had lagged the evening before, leaving me with nothing to do but sit around idly and have the occasional purifying cigarette, had returned in full now. I had, as Alfonso had instructed, created a space within myself for the mushrooms to take hold, and now it was only a matter of hours until they did just that. I gave Elena a call over in Italy, where I knew it was now late afternoon. She was home and, though apparently happy to hear my voice, managed to both disappoint and irritate me with her unenthusiastic reaction to my news about what was about to happen.

"Are you sure that's a good idea?" she asked over the crackly connection. It was the sort of question the people back on shore always cry out to the sailor who has just cast off in search of rich new lands.

After getting off the line with Elena I went up into the kitchen area, and found Alfonso having his breakfast.

"Good news and bad news," he said when he saw me.

"Oh yeah? What's the bad?"

"Turns out I can't be here this afternoon. I've got to go down to Albuquerque to see some people about deeds for some more property I'm thinking of buying. I tried to put it off, but it looks like I really need to go."

My heart sank. After three days of patient preparation, Alfonso was backing out?

"Oh wow, that's terrible. What's the good news?"

"The good news, my friend, is that you don't really need me around anyhow! What you need is the energy of the desert, of the mountain, of the sky; and that stuff's all still right out there. I wasn't coming along on the trip in the sense of taking any mushrooms myself, so in a way having me around would really just be like having a cheeseburger and fries in your stomach. I'd be getting in the way of the essential experience."

I had to admit that I had very much been counting on Alfonso's presence for the adventure. Yet, I could also see the sense in what he was saying. This afternoon I was to enter a world of intense, mystically flavored experience such as I had never known before. I was to have the conceptual foundations of my Western mind-set conclusively rocked—to put on, for the first time ever, the glasses through which the Adults Unlike Other Adults out there saw the world. If Alfonso said I could undergo the experience alone, who was I to doubt him?

Alfonso took his coffee, I took my hot water, and we moved out onto the porch and watched the shadows on his private world depart as the sun rose up behind us.

"A perfect day," said Alfonso, looking out at the big, flat-topped mountain rising gradually up beyond the construction area.

"So where do you think I should go today? I was thinking of climbing to the top of the mountain."

"Yeah," said Alfonso, "that would be great, but the thing is I talked to Zack, and he says it probably wouldn't be such a good idea because of the snakes."

"Snakes?"

"The rattlers like the crevices up there, and it definitely wouldn't be a good idea to run into one while you're on your trip."

This made complete sense, though it was disappointing to think that, with one so close by, I would have to have my experience of nonordinary reality without benefit of an actual mountaintop to look out on the world from.

"How about over by the water?"

Off to the right, beyond the shed where Alfonso's goats lived and the construction area, was a long, straight, narrow waterway separating Alfonso's property from that of his neighbor, a cattle rancher.

"Mmm. That's a good space. I'd say it's just about perfect. So look, here's what you do. Take all the mushrooms at three o'clock. They'll kick in about an hour later, and by that time you should make sure you've found a space with a really good vibe to it—a spot that just *feels* right. Hang out there until the mushrooms really take hold, then see where you feel like letting them take you. There's a lot of energy out there, and it could come at you in any number of ways. Just trust the land and let it lead you."

"So how will I *know* when the mushrooms really take hold?"

"You'll know."

Looking out at the slowly lightening land with the mountain beyond, I felt like an explorer poised on the fringes of a new world. In a few short hours I would be walking off the edge of the conceptual map I had been bounded by for so long and straight into the glossy, Castanedian cactusland of nonordinary consciousness. There, with the meddlesome editing processes of my consensus-mind shut down, I would be privy to the full disclosures of Mind at Large. The landscape would drop its facade of mute physicality and speak to me in a language that I had never heard before but which I would immediately understand all the same. If only it were four o'clock already.

Alfonso finished his coffee and got up. "Come along in here, I've got one more tool to give you for your journey."

We walked into the kitchen and Alfonso rummaged in a big leather saddlebag he sometimes carried around with him. He pulled out a long aluminum cigar tube, opened it, and slid out a neatly rolled joint.

I stared dumbly at it for a moment.

"That's not pot, is it?"

"It is indeed."

"Hmm. I don't really like pot too much. I mean, thanks for getting it for me and everything, but it kind of makes me nervous and stuff when I smoke it."

Alfonso nodded gravely. "Bugs you out, huh?"

"Yeah. I've never really gotten why so many people like it, because it always makes me feel so messed up."

"Well, you will now," Alfonso said, brightening again. "Mushrooms make grass a totally different kind of experience. Everybody gets some of that paranoid stuff with grass sometimes, but you won't with the mushrooms. It'll combine with their energy in a totally different way. If you want a *complete* experience, you need to smoke the whole joint down. Light it up out at the spot you find for yourself, exactly one hour after you've taken all the mushrooms."

"The whole thing? Oh man. Usually only one or two hits gets me totally stoned. Is this weak or something?"

For some reason, Alfonso found this question amusing. "Oh, this stuff isn't weak. Quite the contrary. But I'm telling you, with the mushrooms it's a totally different experience. Remember, these are both organic substances—totally natural. You've worked hard, over the last couple of days, to get in the right physical and mental place for these plants to work on you. Because of that, it'll be like a collaboration between them— between the *spirits* of the two plants—and your own spirit."

There didn't seem to be much to discuss. After all, Carlos had always been suspicious when eating or inhaling whatever mix of ingredients don Juan was dispensing. In the end, though, he had always ended up for the better, so who was I to question Alfonso?

"Okay," I said, putting the joint back in the aluminum tube. "Four o'clock it is."

Alfonso flashed another intense smile.

"There you go! It's going to be an incredible experience. Now, I've got to get ready to split."

Within an hour Alfonso was out the door, leaving me alone for the dry stretch of the lunch hours. Somehow or other they passed. Zack and some of the other ranch regulars came and went, and I chatted a little with them. I went down to my room and picked up the sack of mushrooms, put it down, and picked it up again. I smoked some purifying cigarettes and watched the workers out there in the heat, toiling away like time didn't exist at all. When three o'clock at last arrived, I walked back down to my room, dumped out the sack, and one after another slowly chewed and swallowed the dried goods within. Alfonso had briefed me on the nasty taste of the things, but, perhaps because of my days of preparatory fasting, I didn't find them all that objectionable. One, two, three, four, five, six, seven. . . . Gradually I made my way through the assembled heads and stems until there was just a bit of dust left, which I swallowed too. Remembering Alfonso's council to drink plenty of water, I went to the bathroom and had a glass. Coming back out of the bathroom, my eye settled on one of my half-full bags over in a corner of the room. A book was poking out of it: a miniature volume of paintings by Botticelli. I picked it up and stuck it in my back pocket. Then I collected my cigarettes, a book of matches, and the aluminum cigar tube Alfonso had given me, and walked out the door into the chaparral.

Mind at Large

I looked ahead and saw the mountains there with rocks and forests on them, and from the mountains flashed all colors upward to the heavens. Then I was standing on the highest mountain of them all, and round about beneath me was the whole hoop of the world. And while I stood there I saw more than I can tell and I understood more than I saw; for I was seeing in a sacred manner the shapes of all things in the spirit, and the shape of all shapes as they must live together like one being.

—BLACK ELK

I still had a solid hour to find my power spot, so when I reached the shed where the goats lived I stopped to pass a little more time. I entered the gate, and one by one the goats lowered their bony heads to play a familiar game in which I let them butt against my clenched fist. After a while I left the goats and continued on, giving a wide berth to the area where the laborers were slapping and slathering away at the new buildings— for at this critical moment I didn't want to get engaged in any chitchat with them. I got to the edge of the long canal that divided Alfonso's property from his neighbor's. On the far side, a group of brown and white cows eyed me noncommittally. I set off along the path that bordered the canal.

Passing cow after cow, I walked until the ranch and the toiling laborers were suitably far behind. Up ahead to my left, the sacred mountain rose. I stopped and looked around. I was still next to the canal but cut off from it by a small row of willow-like trees that, thanks to the ever-present water, had grown up amid the arid desert. On the other side of the path from these trees, a single, smooth boulder provided a good support to lean against while I sat and waited. I pulled the Botticelli book from my pocket, sat down, leaned back, and checked the boulder for comfort. The surrounding grass was green and lush thanks to the moisture from the canal, but not damp. The mountain rose up before me with no man-made structures blocking my view. I had found my power spot.

The Woman with Flowers in Her Dress

I began leafing through the book. In *The Doors of Perception*, after spending the morning wandering around in his garden finding hints of heaven among the shrubbery and garden furniture, Huxley had set off by car for a place advertising itself as The World's Biggest Drug Store. There, he had engaged in an amused-yet-horrified inventory of the twentieth century's material accumulations, and when he could take no more had retreated to a small collection of books—one of them featuring paintings by Botticelli. There followed several excited paragraphs explaining how magical this painter's fabrics had looked to Huxley while he was under the influence of mescaline, and I had brought the Botticelli book along in the event that an opportunity arose to check Huxley's claims. I flipped around absently and stopped at my favorite picture in the book, a fold-out of the *Primavera*. One by one, I looked at the figures in the scene: first the three weird, white-gowned women standing all together on the left, then the little blind Cupid hovering overhead, then the woman on the right side with the flowers on her dress and the mysterious smile—a smile that suggested to me some essential, muselike secret about the world, a secret known by her and no one else.

Looking at my watch and seeing that it was now just ten minutes to four, I decided that I was close enough to zero hour. I pulled the aluminum cylinder from my pocket, slid the joint out, lit it, and started smoking. Apparently all the Camels I had gone through with Alfonso had paid off, for though the hot, rich smoke burned my lungs, I managed to hold the stuff in for much longer than I remembered being able to do back in my high school smoking days. I exhaled and took another hit, then another, and another, puffing informally on the joint as though it were just an ordinary cigarette. Usually, on those rare occasions when I found myself smoking marijuana, I was so wary of the negative effects it could have that I never ventured beyond a puff or two. But now, armed with the knowledge that mushrooms rendered its paranoia-inducing effects null and void, smoking the stuff was an entirely different experience. I actually enjoyed taking in lungful after hearty lungful.

Before too long, the joint had burned down close to my fingers. I dropped the butt in the sand, rubbed it out with the toe of my sneaker, and concentrated, looking for the first hints of the new, muted and mellowed marijuana experience that was to come. I picked up the Botticelli book and leafed through it again, stopping one more time at the *Primavera*.

Then I became aware that something was happening.

A curious music was playing somewhere. It sounded a little like someone blowing on a flute—though with a slightly off-kilter quality, and repeating again and again like a skipping record. I also began to notice that my body seemed to be shrinking—or, rather, the inner part of me was shrinking and leaving the outer surface intact, just sitting there against the boulder as if it were the abandoned exoskeleton of a giant insect. This livelier, inner aspect of myself that had shrunk down in size now seemed to disengage itself from the outer part altogether. The fact that it had done so, and the fact that the outer shell continued to just sit there dumbly as if nothing had happened at all, struck me as terribly funny.

Wait a minute. What was so funny? I couldn't remember. From past experiences with marijuana, I knew about this business of laughing at something and then forgetting what you were laughing about even before you had finished doing the actual laughing. The drug tended to make the needle of one's attention drift off track and wander at random down all sorts of absurd imaginative and experiential pathways for what could sometimes feel like a small, private eternity. It usually lasted only a couple of seconds, this drifting off course, but I had never particularly liked the sensation of it—and I was not especially happy that it was happening now, just when I was supposed to be getting my big payoff of more profound and useful insights.

I looked down at the picture of the *Primavera* in the book, but my vision kept drifting away, refusing to stay with the image on the page. I closed my eyes to give them a rest, and to my considerable surprise discovered the entire *Primavera* picture waiting for me there, behind my eyelids—only in a much larger and more vivid form than it had been in my book. I found myself once again zeroing in with particular intensity on the woman on the right side of the picture with the flowers in her dress. The closer I looked, the clearer she became—and yet at the same time I saw that she was actually changing as I looked at her, becoming something or someone other than who she originally was. An impostor.

Then the woman disappeared altogether. Then she was back again, only this time reproduced hundreds of times, like pictures on a huge roll of stamps. She definitely looked different now, though, more like a cartoon and less like the rich, beautiful, otherworldly personage in my book. The annoying flute music was back, playing over and over and over, and all the multiple little *Primavera* women seemed to notice the music too, because they were moving now, marching along in step with it. One of them hiked up her skirt, revealing a black, bushy vagina. The music rose to an even greater intensity and was joined by a sound that was something like that of a vast orchestra of mechanical crickets. Then the *Primavera* women were gone for good and replaced by other images—all of them weird and cartoonlike and oddly empty and alien, yet at the same time familiar too, so that I was slightly angry at myself for not knowing what they meant. They were proceeding at such a speed that it was impossible to hold any of them with my attention for more than a passing instant.

Things were really racing along now, and I began to wish that there were somebody around whom I could talk to—a person I could ask about what was going on and what the meaning of all these absurd images was. Then, almost as if in answer to my wish, another image—bigger and far more definite than all the others—appeared before my eyes. It was so much more real, in fact, that I was genuinely shocked by it. Who on earth was this personage with me all of a sudden, out there in the desert? Was it Mescalito? Krishna? The Buddha? No, it wasn't any of these. With those big black ears and staring eyes and that bright red sorcerer's robe, it could only be one person: it was Mickey Mouse! But what on earth was *he* doing here? I waited for Mickey to lose a little of his frightening reality—to fade away or transform into something else like all the other pictures had. But he didn't. Instead he just continued to stare and smile at me. He smiled and smiled and smiled. Then he pulled a big black gun out of his sorcerer's robes and pointed it right at my face. I waited for the gun to go off but instead in the next instant it was gone, and so was Mickey, and the flute music had stopped too. But the cricket noises were still going, at such a deafening volume that it seemed like they were never, ever going to end.

What the hell was going on? Was this horrible nonsense really what all of Alfonso's meticulous, vision-inducing labors had wrought? How far it was from the experience I had thought I was going to get! After taking Huxley's tasteful encounters with glowing paintings and radiant flower vases so seriously, it was at once humiliating and frightening to find that the hidden levels of my own psyche seemed to be populated with nothing more than mean-spirited cartoons.

That was the bad news. But the good news was that time had been passing, and I now appeared to be coming back to my senses, once again realizing who and where I was and what was happening: specifically, that I was experiencing the simple chemical effect of too many drugs. I took my bearings now, full of gratitude that my brain was once again producing more or less ordinary thought sequences. I realized that I was down on the ground with my face in the sand, and that in order to look around I would have to sit up. But sitting up meant I would have to take my hand out of my mouth. Why on earth was my hand in my mouth? Perhaps I had put it there to keep my teeth from grinding too much. But why were my teeth grinding like that? Because I didn't have any real control over them. My face and my jaw felt like they belonged to someone else, and it seemed unlikely that they would ever return to normal.

What must I look like, lying there? Could anybody see me, curled up in the sand by the big boulder that I had chosen as my power spot? With a burst of effort, I took my hand from my mouth, pushed myself back up into a sitting position, and looked to see if there was any blood or missing fingers. No— they were all there. And next to my fingers was something else—something miraculous. My watch! This, I realized, was my ticket out of this mess—my key to figuring out just exactly how long I had been out here now, and how long it would be before the drugs wore off completely.

I stared at my watch—harder, it felt, than I had ever stared at anything before in my life—and waited for it to mean something. At first the dark oval surface with the shiny little marks on it absolutely refused to hold still—to stop pulsing and twitching and trying to turn into something else. Then, at last, with a wonderful rush of lucidity and good old left-brain, linear understanding, the watch face made sense. Staring at it, I was able to see, and read, and understand exactly what time it was.

Five minutes past four. Fifteen minutes since I had smoked the joint and stubbed it out. The trip, according to Alfonso, should be starting any moment.

A Breeze from Beyond

A few moments later I was back down in the sand again, this time for the long haul. Because my watch, and the regular, humdrum world of consensus reality it was part of, kept going as they normally did for the whole time, I know that I lay out there in the sand by the boulder for another four hours or so.

Somewhere in the third hour the moments of clarity—the realizations of where I was and what was happening, which had been occurring intermittently throughout the adventure—started to grow in frequency. The tide of psychotic cartoon nonsense finally began to withdraw in earnest, and the land around me took up its old familiar garment of solidity and permanence. Rising stiffly, I dusted off my clothes, spat some of the sand out of my mouth, and started back down the path to the ranch. In the sky behind me, the full moon was blocked out by a sheer black front of clouds, and the wind was blowing hard. A storm was approaching, and I realized that if I didn't walk fast I would get caught in it. A great peal of thunder shook down along the desert. The first heavy drops would be here any minute, and I picked up my pace to avoid them. Over by the building site things were quiet, the laborers having gone home hours ago.

Walking along, it was difficult to think very clearly about either what I had just experienced or what I thought about it. One thing was clear though: after months of plotting and maneuvering, I had finally succeeded in getting an initial audience with Emperor Hun Tun—with the vast and measureless chaos that lay just behind the humdrum, reassuring world of surface meanings and surface comforts in which I normally lived, and with which I had for so long been so dissatisfied. A door had opened, and I had felt, for a moment, the breeze from a place lying genuinely beyond.

But it had not been what I expected, that other place. Even though I didn't want to admit it and was in fact already looking for ways of telling myself otherwise, it wasn't the place that I had wanted it to be at all.

THE REAL MAGICIAN

The Moral of the Story

Don Juan and don Genaro looked at each other. There was something so sad about their look.

"In my journey to Ixtlan I find only phantom travelers," he said softly.

I looked at don Juan. I had not understood what don Genaro had meant.

"Everyone Genaro finds on his way to Ixtlan is only an ephemeral being," don Juan explained. "Take you, for instance. You are a phantom. Your feelings and your eagerness are those of people. That's why he says that he encounters only phantom travelers on his journey to Ixtlan."

I suddenly realized that don Genaro's journey was a metaphor.

"Your journey to Ixtlan is not real then," I said.

"It is real!" don Genaro interjected. "The travelers are not real."

—CARLOS CASTANEDA, *JOURNEY TO IXTLAN*

The purpose of the final chapter of a Life Manual—especially a Life Manual that features a plot—is to leave the reader with a moral: a statement of the lessons learned from all that has occurred in its pages. Of course, such morals differ depending on the Life Manual in question. Some wrap up with the promise that life really does—at least sometimes—work out the way it's supposed to, while others strike a more indeterminate note. *Zen and the Art of Motorcycle Maintenance,* for example, ends with the arrival of Robert Pirsig and his son on the coast of California after a cross-country voyage that has taken the reader on a parallel psychological journey into Pirsig's past and the troubled quest for truth that unfolded in the course of it. "Trials never end," Pirsig wrote in that book's famous last lines, where tragedy and triumph mingle together inextricably. "Unhappiness and misfortune are bound to occur as long as people live, but there is a feeling now, that was not there before, and is not just on the surface of things, but penetrates all the way through: We've won it. It's going to get better now. You can sort of tell these things."

Like many of the more profound Life Manuals out there, Pirsig's book leaves us satisfied, but with a deep sense of ambiguity all the same. Is the author's optimism warranted? And does he in fact really mean it about things getting better, or is he only bravely pretending?

The Price of Wisdom

Any Life Manual worth its salt—even the most optimistic—will have *something* to say about life's essential shortcomings. After all, that was where the appeal of the Adult Unlike Other Adults came from to begin with. Knowing in advance that life tends to be something of a gyp, the Adult Unlike Other Adults steers a course around its ordinary geography, in order to ultimately arrive at a better place than the one where most people end up.

And yet, it's often not quite as simple as that either. For as it turns out, there are losses to be suffered, and prices to be paid, even when one manages to find and tread the path of the masters. For all the grandeur and mystery of the way of wisdom, it often seemed, from my perspective at least, to be marked with a deep and unignorable melancholy—a sadness at its very heart. So it is that today's Life Manual reader can ultimately discover—to his or her chagrin—that by avoiding the disappointments of ordinary adulthood, a man or woman of wisdom doesn't really end up completely free from unhappiness and disappointment after all. Instead, he or she only ends up trading one kind for another.

What was the cause of this sadness that so often seemed to come along with getting wise? More than anything else it was the distance—the feeling of separation—that grew up between the wise person and the rest of the world. From the solitary Siddhartha sitting on the banks of that ever-changing river of his over in India, to the Japanese Zen poets who wandered alone among all those endless valleys and mountains shrouded in mist and clouds, to Carlos and don Juan out in the Sonora, the picture my wisdom manuals left me with was often a noble but also an achingly lonely one as well. Sure, there was the occasional warm and fuzzy Life Manual that celebrated ordinary life and interpersonal relationships, but even these often ended with the sudden, sad assertion that things like love and friendship were still nothing but fleeting consolations. At the heart of the great majority of my Life Manuals there lay a chill core of cosmic loneliness—a heartbreaking insistence on the transiency of life and the inevitability of loss and disappointment. To truly see into the nature of the world, my Life Manuals again and again suggested, meant ending up a stranger to that world, and all the things and people within it, forever after.

Minus and Plus

No one was more talented at painting this sort of picture than Castaneda. In *Journey to Ixtlan*, don Juan wrapped things up with a long and detailed description of the piercing isolation that inevitably accompanied a walker of the path of wisdom. All the joys and consolations of ordinary people, Castaneda made plain, simply had to be left in the ditch by such an individual. To become wise, according to don Juan—and according to people like Nicky and his Buddhists too, as far as I could see— meant enduring what in the end became a single-minded and profoundly solitary journey. This journey had its joys, certainly, but by and large they were of a decidedly stark and windswept nature—far indeed from the cozy consolations that made ordinary folk think, at least for moments, that they were happy. In fact, in books like Castaneda's, the Adult Unlike Other Adults became *so* unlike other adults that he sometimes seemed to cease being human altogether.

Not that I had forgotten about the existence of the *via positiva*—the wisdom path that aggressively made use of life's pleasures and consolations—and its champions like Henry Miller. Yet after a while one had to admit that for all its seductiveness, this path too was disappointing. For all his tireless endorsements of life and the joys it held, a dedicated reader of Miller's books ultimately couldn't help but notice that he himself was actually an extraordinarily tormented fellow. Yes, Miller had had a great time in life, sleeping with scores of women, wandering the streets of exotic cities, swimming by moonlight in far-flung oceans, smoking cigarettes, writing books, and talking far into the small hours with his fellow masters of the *via positiva*. But it wasn't as though all that fun had rescued him from suffering misery and heartbreak as well (usually, though not exclusively, at the hands of some woman or other).

Even though he had done a remarkable job of accepting *all* the stuff that happened to him, both good and bad, just as a real Artist of Life was supposed to, it sometimes seemed that the Fates had taken special pleasure in making Miller squirm as payment for having dared to do so. Closing one of his relentlessly optimistic yet misery-laden life reminiscences, one sometimes couldn't help but wonder whether, if it took *that* much work to be positive about life, it wasn't a whole lot simpler just to be negative instead.

A Sad, Single Road

Life is an island in a sea of solitude and isolation.

—KAHLIL GIBRAN, *VISIONS OF THE PROPHET*

So it was that, although there were *supposed* to be the two roads to wisdom—the *via positiva* and the *via negativa*—it was definitely starting to look like there was really only one, and that it was a path of tears no matter how much you might try to pretend that it wasn't. Moreover, not only were isolation and sadness inevitable all along that way, but even the destination itself—the exalted end zone of genuine, bona fide, surefire wisdom—seemed all but guaranteed to be a place of loneliness too. Perhaps it was even the loneliest place of all.

The more lost in the Life Manual supermarket I became, the more this sense of the ultimate isolation that haunted the roads to wisdom began to wear at me. Was there a way of getting wise that didn't entail such deep and lasting loneliness? Did realizing my identity with the cosmos really mean losing all faith in the joys of ordinary life and ordinary human relationships—of becoming an even more odd and isolated person than I already was? Did I simply have to get used to the idea, driven home by all the endless images of drifting clouds and flowing rivers in my Life Manuals, that nothing ever stayed as it was, that all events and all relationships eventually passed on like so much wind and water? Sure, all that cloud and river stuff was pretty to read about, but the thing was that when you really stopped and thought about it all for a while, it was downright depressing too. After immersing oneself in Nothingness for long enough, a person really couldn't help but start to hanker for a little in the way of Somethingness instead.

A Tear in the Curtain

When a man goes astray from the path to Brahman, he has missed both lives, the worldly and the spiritual. He has no support anywhere. Is he not lost, as a broken cloud is lost in the sky?

—BHAGAVAD GITA

"Well . . . ? How'd it go?"

Alfonso looked me up and down, as if checking for actual changes in my physical person. We were down in the kitchen the following morning, and he was seeing me for the first time since my adventure because by the time he had gotten back from Albuquerque the night before I was already sound asleep. I hesitated before giving an answer.

"It was kind of . . . different than I thought it would be."

"Yeah? How so? Did you walk around, feel the energies in the desert?"

"I didn't really walk around. I kind of just stayed in one place."

I thought of telling Alfonso about lying on the sand with my hand stuck in my mouth, of Mickey Mouse pointing a gun at me and the *Primavera* woman lifting up her dress, but somehow none of it really seemed appropriate. Finally, I decided simply to soft-pedal the whole business and pretend that nothing much had happened out in the desert at all. After the massive buildup, Alfonso would no doubt be disappointed at not getting a good story about visionary adventures and timeless insights. But I knew that if I downplayed the topic long enough, Alfonso would eventually move his ever-enthusiastic attention on to other things.

And that was just what happened. After a day or so of noncommittal answers from me, Alfonso shifted his interest to other topics, and soon it was almost as if the Great Mushroom Experiment had never happened at all. We resumed our old schedule of movies and restaurants, of driving here and there, of chatting and smoking the occasional Camel and just generally having a pleasant time.

But something was wrong now. For though I wasn't sure whether Alfonso noticed it or not, it was clear to me that I wasn't quite the same person I had been before eating all those confounded mushrooms. I couldn't really put my finger on what it was that was different about me, but *something* definitely was. It was as if someone had left a back door open in the house of my mind, and a wind from outside was moving through all of the rooms, slamming doors, blowing things off tables, and lowering the general temperature. It was a weird, wounded feeling—one I had never experienced before. And, unfortunately, it was a decidedly uncosmic one as well. It wasn't like I was One with the universe or anything good like that. It was more that the fragility of my mind had been made apparent in a way that it had never been before. That boring old feeling of ordinary consciousness—the one that I had always taken as much for granted as the ground I walked on—now revealed itself to be altogether less firm and reliable than I had thought it was. The seemingly solid barrier separating me from the vast, roiling chaos of Hun Tun was, in fact, I now realized, really as fragile as a spiderweb. The slightest pressure could rend it, and when that happened, the things that came into view were not necessarily wild and interesting and cos-mic—or even pleasant. In short, I realized for the first time in my life that it really was possible to go crazy—and that to do so was not so much fun after all.

It wasn't like some of my Life Manuals hadn't tried to tell me as much ahead of time. Pirsig certainly hadn't made his bout with madness sound any too pleasant. And for all the bubbling enthusiasm of Huxley's mescaline endorsements, he had also added a sufficient number of provisos about entering hell instead of heaven, the brush of the wing of madness, and so forth, to give a person second thoughts about the whole busi-ness. But somehow or other—probably because these bits didn't interest me as much as the other, more positive mate-rial—I had ignored Huxley's warnings and simply concentrated on the good stuff he described. After all, I had reasoned, even if I did end up in hell instead of heaven, a visit there would no doubt be more interesting and educational than being stuck in plain old ordinary life.

Well, it *had* been educational, after a fashion; but I was at a loss to say just what it was I had learned. All I knew for sure was that, on some new level that I wasn't at all used to experiencing, I felt strangely diminished by my adventure. Against expecta-tion, I had come away from my initial interview with Emperor Hun Tun as less, rather than more, of the person I had origi-nally been.

Vision Problems

There were also some more concrete indications that my Big Trip had left me more eroded than enlightened. A day or so after it, Alfonso and I went to the only movie left in Santa Fe that we hadn't seen yet: *Endless Love,* starring Brooke Shields. As soon as the film began, I noticed that something was wrong with the picture. Strange little spots jumped into the air when I looked up at the screen, then drifted down like snowflakes in a child's toy snow globe. At first I thought these small, leaping imperfections were part of the film, but it soon became obvious that they weren't up there on the screen at all, but in my eyes.

The next day Alfonso and I drove up into the mountains and had a picnic on the property of some friends of his, playing croquet on a deep green lawn fed by a set of sprinklers. As usual it was a beautiful day, the sky an endless ocean of blue set about with the occasional massive cumulus cloud. And each time I raised my eyes to look at that sky I saw it through a virtual storm of those dancing little imperfections—the same ones that had floated and jumped about on the movie screen, only even more of them now. It was as if the liquid of my eyes had been stirred up—muddied somehow, like the waters of a lake. Chaos. The wild havoc of Hun Tun that I had so long been seeking. It was actually inside me now.

I didn't mention the little swimming spots in my eyes to Alfonso, but between them and that odd, empty, diminished feeling the mushrooms had left me with, my performance as a fun guest was definitely suffering. With the structure provided by the mushroom vision quest gone and my spirits troubled by all these strange new physical and psychological side effects, our daily outings now had noticeably less pep to them. Before too many more days had passed, I realized that, easy as it would have been to linger there longer, it was time for me to leave the ranch and continue with my journey west. One morning some two weeks after getting there, I climbed back into the Sunbird, and with Alfonso's best wishes, I set off on the next and final portion of my trip.

The Big Picture

One of the best things about getting to the end of a Life Manual is the no-nonsense honesty that can greet one there. Being by nature slim and full of deep insights, Life Manuals are generally more straightforward than other books anyhow, but in their final pages the writer will sometimes take even greater efforts to drop all coyness and really show his cards. It's a last look at the Big Picture—both of life and of wisdom's ideal role in life, as the author has come to understand it.

In the case of this Life Manual, the Big Picture runs more or less as follows. Ordinary life, as lived by the "mass of men," as Thoreau called them—the folk who never bother to seek out a larger knowledge of things—is inevitably a disappointing event. Another life, another path, is out there, waiting for those who possess the requisite wit and energy to find it, and unless that other path is found, one's prospects in life are feeble indeed. However, for all that we might struggle and manipulate to think otherwise, it turns out that this other life—this alternate way walked by the Adult Unlike Other Adults—has its disappointments too. For like it or not, the way of wisdom—if you listened to a Buddhist, or a Yaqui sorcerer like don Juan, or even an Artist of Life like Henry Miller when he was in one of his downcast moods—brings with it a certain unfathomable melancholy.

Was this really the way it had to work?

The Highway and the Service Road

Though I didn't know it back then, I was eventually to discover that there had actually been plenty of times and places in which the task of getting wise—and in particular the first brush with the world of wisdom that so often happens during a person's teenage years—didn't have to be quite the isolated, depressing, and disorienting experience that it had ended up becoming for me. For in fact, most of the world's vast stock of wisdom traditions never told all the regular people out there living their ordinary lives that they were making a dreadful mistake by doing so at all. Even when a wisdom tradition has exceptionally harsh things to say about the shortcomings of the human situation—and all of them do in some spots—in the great majority of cases these remarks are not intended to actually stop a person in his tracks and keep him from living the life he has been given. Instead, the intent is to place that "normal" existence within a wider context—to show it in the light of the larger, more powerful, and more mysterious universe of spiritual realities that surrounds and upholds it.

It is precisely because most people throughout the world and throughout history have so keenly believed that everyday life depends upon such a larger landscape of spiritual meanings that a direct encounter with wisdom has always been such an important part of becoming an adult. However, for most people most of the time, this *encounter* has been just that: a brief, controlled introduction, followed by a return to ordinary life. Even when this first brush with the spiritual world was deeply traumatic and unsettling—as it could indeed be for the members of many tribal cultures, for example—the trauma tended to be momentary and was not intended to so shock the wisdom pilgrim that he or she lost all touch with the more mundane realities and responsibilities of his or her life.

As Krishna was always telling Arjuna, getting wise doesn't mean becoming hopelessly lost in some other dimension of reality, nor does wisdom necessarily ask all who encounter it to drop everything and refuse to live as others do from there on out (though a certain select minority do in fact choose this option). At its simplest and best, getting wise just means getting a new—and more comprehensive—angle of vision on what life is really about, and then using that larger vision as a source of strength and inspiration when one is back among the assorted pleasures, pains, frustrations, and contradictions of the ordinary world. So it is, for example, that in the Zen ox-herding pictures, the wisdom pilgrim who sets off into the woods to capture the ox of enlightenment doesn't stay lost in the woods *forever*, but eventually makes his way back into the village he started out from, the ox now tranquilly in tow behind him. In such cases, the path walked by the "mass of men" and the path walked by the Adult Unlike Other Adults aren't so hopelessly separate from each other at all, but instead weave back and forth, crossing and even overlapping, constantly.

At its best, I eventually came to think, real wisdom is something like the service road of a highway. Rather than calling every last person away from their role in the mundane, nuts-and-bolts world of human life and human problems, wisdom's job is to run along parallel with that life, flashing in and out of view. Just because the service road is vital to the functioning of the highway doesn't mean—as sometimes seems to be happening today—that everyone should forsake that highway altogether and crowd onto the service road instead. For most people most of the time, just being aware that the service road is out there is enough. For as Lao-tzu said of the Tao, it is sometimes most useful when no one sees it at all.

That may have been the way wisdom functioned in the times and places when it was really working, but during those teenage years of mine when I was so determinedly on its trail, it was obvious that something different was going on. For far from helping me learn who and what I was at the deepest levels of my being and then allowing me to get on with the business of finding my place in the world, my wisdom quest instead ended up taking me in the exact opposite direction. Getting ever more dazed and confused with each new leg of my wisdom journey, I ended up less sure about what life was about, and less sure of what role, if any, I might stand a chance of playing in it, than I had been when I started out.

At Loose Ends on the West Coast

California showed up before I knew it. I spent the night at a ramshackle little motel just west of the border town of Needles, and the next day drove on until I hit the coast at San Luis Obispo. I took a right, and moved up the lazy, meandering length of Route 1, with the Pacific keeping me company all the way, until I got to Big Sur—a spot rendered mythical in my mind by the fact that Henry Miller had lived and written there for so many years. The place was every bit the primordial wonderland that Miller had prepared me to expect. But it was also clearly a rather exclusive place, and my plans of lingering there for a while were compromised by the extremely stiff rates of the few available lodgings. The whole point of unspoiled spots like Big Sur was, of course, that they didn't have things like 7-Elevens and Motel 6's to mess them up. Unfortunately, this lack of modern blight made things inconvenient for a half-baked bohemian voyager like myself. I pulled into a campground, where for nine dollars I was allowed to sleep in the Sunbird for the night without fear of being disturbed by police or any of those serial killers I knew California was famous for. Waking up cramped and unrested, I drove back to one of the overlooks off Route 1 where you could stare down and see the waves breaking, distant and inaudible, against the rocky line of coast. I smoked a couple of cigarettes and pondered what to do next.

Now that Alfonso and his ranch were behind me, I was back in the feeling of being a definite outsider—someone for whom America, despite all its vast and scenic terrain spread out right beneath my feet, was still something of a closed book. Once again, the problem seemed to lie in large part with the limbo-like nature of my financial state. For those either richer or poorer than me, I realized, a certain code of engagement with the country was available. If, for example, you had the gump-tion to be one of those ragged, backpacking, hippie-holdover types crowding either side of Route 1 with their thumbs raised to the passing cars, then America could be experienced at extreme close range. Or, if you had the dough, you could join the tribe of wealthy people packed into the lodges set up here and there at the especially scenic spots along the way. But if, like me, you were stuck in the middle—too rich to be poor and too poor to be rich—it was tough to say exactly what you could do.

Life Versus Theory

Before too long I left the glorious but hermetic environs of Big Sur behind and wound my way through more looping miles of Route 1, the Pacific rumbling off to my left, and the tranquil, green-gold hills of the land of milk and honey stretching away to my right. By that afternoon, I found myself at a filling station staring across a body of water at the city of San Francisco—the place from which Alan Watts, just a few short decades before, had commenced spreading the word about the Eternal Now, the nonexistence of the ego, and becoming one with the uni-verse. Despite Alfonso's endless generosity with me, my cash reserves were now very low, and while in theory it seemed like it might be fun to enter the city and drive around, I couldn't imagine what I would actually do once I got over there. Sure, I could track down the famous City Lights bookstore and add some more Life Manuals to my collection, but to be buying books about life now—at this crucial moment in which I was so obviously supposed to be actually *living* instead of merely theorizing about living—seemed overly evasive. And in any case, a major city would surely drain me of the last of my cash faster than the open highway would, and I still had Portland to think about. Lame as I knew it was to do so, I pulled back onto the highway and kept heading north.

Hitchhikers had been plentiful on either side of the road ever since passing through Big Sur, and I now decided to goose up my spontaneity level by picking one of them up. The first to appear after I made this decision was a tall Native American fellow, not too much older than me, who once he was in the passenger seat shocked me with how much he resembled a younger version of the Big Indian character in the film version of *One Flew Over the Cuckoo's Nest*. Though not mute, my new passenger soon proved sufficiently silent for me to wonder whether I should have picked him up in the first place. As the absurdly dramatic coast-line scenery crashed and shone and glittered around us, and as I did my best to appreciate it all in spite of those irritating little spots that continued to swim around in my eyes, my new passenger kept his counsel, staring out at the passing spectacle without comment. When he was finally out of the car a few hours north of San Francisco, I breathed a mild sigh of relief and headed on.

Montana to McLean

I made it as far as Portland and lingered there a couple of days. Now and then, while driving to and from my base at a Motel 6 on the outskirts of town, I saw signs pointing the way to Seattle. But with my cash reserves gone and what I figured were probably way too many receipts from the American Express card now on the floor of the car, I soon decided to get on the highway heading east, toward home. In Miles City, Montana, after a long, straight trek through unending fields of summer wheat at seventy-five miles an hour, I slept soundly in yet another Motel 6. At some point in the course of that day, looking in my rearview mirror, I had caught a glimpse of what must have been the northern outskirts of the Rockies. The sharp peaks, etched with a pinkish line of snow along the top, had the picture-perfect look of a postcard—and framed in my little rearview mirror, they might just as well have been one.

When I awoke the next morning in Miles City, I did so with the distinct feeling that, though I was only in Montana and still more than a thousand miles away from where I had started, it was time to wrap up this road-trip business and get home. I climbed back into the Sunbird, got out on the great American highway, and drove with the newfound resolve of one who knows that, for better or worse, his journey is done. North Dakota, Minnesota, Wisconsin, Indiana, Ohio. One after another, through that day and into the night and through the next day as well, the states of my country slid by, their towns and cities marked on one green highway sign after another. I drove and drove and drove, stopping only for coffee and gas, until at last, some thirty-six hours after pulling onto the road in Miles City, I found myself turning the Sunbird into the driveway I had started out from in McLean.

It was amazing. Just under three weeks after setting out, I was back from my great American road trip, lying on my bed in the room I had left behind, staring at the ceiling and finding it curiously difficult to get to sleep after all those hours awake at the wheel. What had changed as a result of my voyage? My father's American Express bill would be a little larger than usual next month, the Sunbird had some extra miles on it; but beyond that there seemed to be little that I could put my finger on. Little, that is, except those odd new squiggly imperfections inside my eyes. At the optometrist's a few days after my return, I learned that they were called "floaters," and that they were nothing to worry about. In fact, the doctor told me, a lot of

people got them. They could show up for any number of reasons, but one of the things that tended to make them appear
abruptly was an intense psychological disturbance of some sort.

"They're just something you'll have to get used to," the doctor said at the end of the visit.

Nor were they the only consequence of my trip that would
require some getting used to, for I now had to make my peace
with the fact that my quest—my year-plus of intensive search-
ing for that Larger Vision that all my wisdom books had been
telling me so much about for so long—was really over. I had
returned from all my journeys to the place I had started out
from, and against all expectation, I was *still* not enlightened.
The small self had been knocked from its position of command, the psychic floodgates had been opened, and the waters
of Mind at Large had rushed in, just as I had for so long hoped
they would. But the result of that flood was altogether different
from what I had supposed it would be. Like it or not, I had to
face the fact that I had come home from my journey not as
more of a genuine, full-fledged, ready-for-life person than I had
been when I started out, but less of one.

Wisdom Later On

Not that my quest for wisdom was at a *complete* end, however. It
went on for a few more months still, and even a few more
years. In fact, though it never again took on quite the crazy
focus that it did during those initial days, it never went away
entirely at all.

Over time, though, its contours changed, and quite consid-
erably. After my teens, a gradual distancing process commenced—one in which I became less and less taken up with
actually getting wise, and more interested in trying to understand the workings of my initial desire to do so. The old ideals

of wisdom, and of the Adult Unlike Other Adults at their core, became *ideas* now—subjects I could examine from a distance, and about which I could have my doubts as well as my positive feelings.

In other words I got jaded, just as I had always feared I would.

But not *that* jaded. For though I did lose much of my initial naive faith that enlightenment—enlightenment of the definitive and earth-shattering sort that so many of my wisdom masters had described to me—was just around the corner waiting to pounce, I didn't lose my whole passion for the basic promise that wisdom held out. One question in particular stayed in my mind. What exactly was it that had gone wrong with my own wisdom quest—what had made my initial teenage days as a wisdom seeker as oddly inauspicious as they were?

As I continued to ask this question on and off over the years, a number of interesting facts emerged. To begin with, I realized that those solitary, boneheaded, and highly inconclusive adventures of mine were not really so unique at all. Though I didn't know it while it was actually going on, it turned out that my wisdom odyssey was, in its weird way, all but stereotypical. The things that had gone wrong for me were pretty much the same things that had gone wrong for countless others—products, like me, of the uniquely wisdom-starved yet wisdom-obsessed culture into which I had been born. Of course, there were some details that did separate me from the pack here and there. My quest had been a little more bizarre than average in some spots, a little more lame in others; but by and large it was all standard issue. The mistakes, the mishaps, the misunderstandings had all happened for many, many others as they had for me.

Reappraising the Masters

In our society . . . the elders are missing.

—LOUISE CARUS MAHDI

The more I learned about how typical my own failed wisdom adventures had been, the more I also learned about how vastly more successful the quest for wisdom had been in times and places other than mine. From Eskimos to Aborigines, and even among those stodgy old Jews, Christians, and Moslems, whose beliefs and rituals I hadn't been able to bring myself to study back in World Religions, the encounter with wisdom had once really and truly helped people—particularly young people on the verge of adulthood—to live better lives than they would have otherwise. To understand why my own wisdom quest had gone off the tracks, I realized it was necessary to address why the wisdom-getting adventure in general had come to such a sorry pass these days—why, for all its huge popularity, it was now often little more than a parody of what it once had been.

In order to seek out this explanation, I eventually found myself returning to the works of my old teachers and studying them with fresh eyes. I also did something which, during the years of my initial tutelage under them, would have been unthinkable. I began examining the actual lives of these individuals—the day-to-day goings-on of the genuine, flesh-and-blood people who had been responsible for creating the figure of the Adult Unlike Other Adults as I had first encountered it in my wisdom books. As a teenager, I was always more than ready to savor the shortcomings of most of the adults around me, but not those of my actual wisdom masters. Being my heroes, these individuals were beyond criticism, and I had treated any details about their personal lives that had happened to come my way with a resolute and pious disinterest. Now, it was just these nuts-and-bolts details that I went in search of.

Before long, and with very little effort, I accumulated an astonishing amount of ugly information. Scholarly and biographical investigation of my heroes had been proceeding apace, and this material, as I gradually came across it, was full of sobering revelations. I learned that Carlos Castaneda, the steely-eyed walker of the sorcerer's path, was a man with a mission all right, but that this mission was very different indeed from what I had originally thought it was. Wise old don Juan, it was now agreed by nearly all who were still interested in the matter, was a fabrication, as were all the talking coyotes, luminous eggs, and glowing green fogs that he and Carlos had tangled with out in the wastes of the Sonora. In fact, it seemed that Castaneda had most likely dreamed up his wily Yaqui instructor out of whole cloth in the depths of the U.C.L.A. Anthropology Library, and had foisted him upon the world simply for laughs, or to gain mere fame and fortune, or for some other more mysterious reason known only to him.

Disappointments Everywhere

In this new look at my old masters, Castaneda turned out to be the tip of the iceberg. Another figure from the past who now revealed his true and very surprising colors was Alan Watts, the man of the Eternal Now who had so charmed and energized me with his rhapsodies on the Tao. The wise and watery Watts, it turned out, had in real life been a hard-drinking, chain-smoking, ego-toting man of the world: an all-too-human pleasure hound who was happy with the suchness of the Now largely because he could always count on a drink, a smoke, and a busty grad student fascinated with his grasp of the mysteries to fill it up.

So good was Watts at writing about the Tao and related matters—so adept was he at providing the sort of shiny, reader-friendly wisdom packet that publishers and booksellers go nuts for these days—that the deep personal torment he seems to have been in for much of the last portion of his life went unnoticed, or at least ignored, by most of the people around him. For it was not that Watts was such a bad guy. He was simply a well-meaning, highly talented, but flawed individual, whose imperfections led him ultimately to become a victim of the excessive adulation heaped on wisdom masters in our age of wisdom-as-product. Ultimately, that adulation destroyed him.

The story of Watts's later years is a deeply sad one. As it turned out, the man who counseled me with such eloquence on the need to overcome all feelings of duality between my single, solitary self and the great world beyond could barely bring himself to spend a night alone. The man who prescribed freedom from all attachment to forms and concepts chugged vodka from the bottle, and in his final days sometimes actually lost consciousness momentarily at speaking engagements (a habit that, remarkably, often went either unnoticed by his adoring audience or else was read as a momentary lapse into samadhi). Toward the end of his life, one of Watts's children is reported to have directly asked him why he insisted on drinking as much as he did when it was so clearly destroying him. Stepping out for a moment from behind the edifice of Enlightened One that had been hammered up all around him, Watts answered simply that when he didn't drink, he didn't like himself. The perfect sage for our age of packaged wisdom, Watts died of alcohol-related problems in 1973, at the age of fifty-eight.

Dirt

Would you know whence it is that so many false spirits have
appeared in the world, who have deceived themselves and
others with false fire and false light, laying claim to information, illumination and openings of the divine life, particularly
to do wonders under extraordinary calls from God? It is this:
they have turned to God without turning from themselves;
would be alive to God before they are dead to their own
nature. Now religion in the hands of self, or corrupt nature,
serves only to discover vices of a worse kind than in nature left
to itself.

—WILLIAM LAW

So many youths, and not a finished man!

—EMERSON

From one to another to another, there was just about always
something in the biographies of my Life Manual masters to
give me pause for thought. This guru was a drunk; that Zen
master was a pedophile; this swami was on the lam for income
tax fraud; that Native American sage wasn't really a sage, or
even a Native American, at all. It went on and on and on.

Even when a popular wisdom figure's biography showed
him or her to be a genuinely wise, genuinely remarkable individual—as certainly happened with frequency too—kinks in
their story often showed up in other ways. The Sioux medicine
man Black Elk, for example—next to Castaneda probably the
single most popular voice of Native American wisdom in
recent decades—turned out to have spent the latter half of his
life as an enthusiastic convert to Catholicism. Because this
embrace of the white man's religion went against Black Elk's

image as a beleaguered champion of pre-Colombian spiritual-
ity (so memorably, if not altogether accurately, portrayed in
Black Elk Speaks), these highly significant later chapters of his
life story were left almost entirely out of the Life Manuals that
made use of his teachings. As a result the life of one of America's most genuine and remarkable wise men became wrapped
up in an essential evasion—one that Black Elk himself would
never have wanted or encouraged.

All these pieces of evidence pointed to the same conclusion.
The experience of having lost touch with the true domains of
wisdom—of going in search of Emperor Hun Tun in the wrong
way and coming back with all the wrong goods—was not peculiar to me alone, nor was it even confined to all the other
bumble-headed young wisdom seekers like me out there. The
problem was at work with the masters themselves.

If seeking and finding real wisdom is something that people
have always done—if doing so is in fact inseparable from being
human—then it was clear that my culture had lost its real faith
in this mysterious skill, and was instead just going through the
motions. Wisdom-as-*product* had taken the place of wisdom-as-
genuine-*process*, and in the course of this transformation, the
whole vast, infinitely complex and mysterious question of what
really constitutes human fallibility and human perfection had
been tossed aside as well. The more that people fell out of contact with the living reality of wisdom, and the more they lost
the ability to engage that reality in a truly meaningful way, the
more they seemed to be compensating for this by electing
pleasingly flashy but blatantly flawed individuals into the office
of Wise One and worshiping them blindly for as long as they
could keep up the act. The habit had become so entrenched
that many of these individuals—Castaneda and Watts among
them—ended up being worshiped long after they had deliv-

ered more than sufficient evidence to their followers that they were really just regular people after all.

A Final Lesson from Huxley

In their different ways, all my old masters ended up teaching me something about wisdom after all. From people like Watts, along with much that was in fact insightful and valuable, I learned about the dangers of a wisdom that is too sweet and easy; while from people like Castaneda I learned an equal amount about the pitfalls of a wisdom that is too willfully diffi-cult and self-servingly otherworldly. But of all my less-than-perfect early masters, the one who probably ended up teaching me the most about our increasingly flawed modern relationship with wisdom—what it is, what it was, and what it could per-haps once again become if we could only remember how to honor and address it properly—was Aldous Huxley.

Huxley's was a life divided, quite neatly, in two. The bril-liant satirical novelist and social critic of the twenties and thir-ties was an all but entirely different creature from Huxley the wisdom-hunting mystic. The end of that first incarnation and the slow birth of the second can be roughly dated to Huxley's move to southern California just before the Second World War. By the mid-sixties, the Huxley of the earlier writing—from *Point Counter Point* to *Brave New World*—had been all but completely eclipsed by the writer on display in works like *The Perennial Philosophy* and *The Doors of Perception*. Even though many of his original readers scorned what they saw as a slide into softheadedness, it turned out to be this second incarnation that Huxley's new country of residence really needed to hear from. For the last ten years of his life, more or less beginning with the publication of *The Doors of Perception* in 1954, Huxley's fame as a wisdom voice grew steadily, so that by the early sixties his was probably the single most resonant name for a young, or not-so-young, person out to learn about and perhaps become an Adult Unlike Other Adults. It was also during this stretch, as Huxley's public role of wisdom master was cemented, that his actual life became a series of marvelously, sometimes chillingly, specific illustrations of what the encounter with wisdom really demands.

Along with chaos, the concept of Hun Tun stands, in Taoist thought, for life in its totality—the whole package, as opposed to just this or that particular bit of it. (The noodles in wonton soup actually derive their name from this term. Wonton soup is really Hun Tun soup because the noodles floating in it encase a mixed-up mush of various and sometimes seemingly incompatible ingredients, just as life itself does.) The Taoist philosophers who came up with the concept of Hun Tun were the same ones who never tired of insisting that to live life properly meant learning to say yes to it—to accept all that came one's way. Without this willingness to completely give oneself to life, and in turn to receive all of what life has to give, the reconciliation of the urge to love life with the equally powerful temptation to hate it (a reconciliation that, at heart, is as good a definition of true wisdom as any) can never really take place.

Such was the reconciliation that Huxley, in the final decade of his life, was asked to make.

An Interview with the Emperor

The initial movement in the strangely orchestrated series of encounters between Huxley and Emperor Hun Tun came when Maria, his wife of decades, was diagnosed with breast cancer in 1952. Even as Huxley was examining his lawn furniture through the lens of mescaline in the spring of the following year, the disease was well advanced, and by the summer of

1954 her case was declared terminal. Interestingly enough, Maria's first concern upon hearing this news was to keep it from her husband. "Aldous did not want to know that Maria was dying," Huxley biographer David King Dunaway quotes Huxley's sister-in-law Juliette saying of him at this time. "And Maria did not want him to know. Of course he knew. But he pushed it away. Didn't want to talk about it. He was protecting himself from a truth which was unbearable."

Huxley's mother had already succumbed to cancer. To him the disease stood, in fact, for everything that was frightening and unknowable about the universe—the darker side of Hun Tun's domain made manifest. Faced as he now was with the true contours of that domain in all their sublime and terrible actuality, it is understandable that America's most influential and arguably most brilliant seeker of truth with a capital *T* should find himself waffling. And waffle he did. Huxley now took to insisting that his wife's physical problems were due to lumbago, arthritis, exhaustion—anything but their true source. For Huxley as for so many of today's wisdom gurus, truth as lived and truth as written about were not always the same beasts.

No Respect for Boundaries

Fire catches up with everything, in time.
—HERACLEITUS (TRANSLATED BY GUY DAVENPORT)

Huxley continued to do his best to avoid the issue up until Maria's very last days—alternately hoping or pretending that none of it was really happening. Finally, when her imminent death was so obvious that avoidance was simply no longer a possibility, Huxley shifted gears. Administering a dose of LSD in her final hours, Huxley guided Maria into the next world using passages from *The Tibetan Book of the Dead.* In March of

1956 Huxley married again, this time to Laura Archera, a woman some twenty years his junior, whom he had met in the course of his investigations of alternative healing. In July of the same year, the two took up residence in a large house in the Hollywood Hills. Soon after the wedding, at a visit to the dentist, Huxley complained of a painful lump on his tongue. After a biopsy indicated a malignancy, Huxley was advised to have a third of his tongue removed—a singularly horrifying prospect for a man who had built a life around the word, both written and spoken. Huxley and Laura left the hospital without even pausing to check out. Less radical treatment methods were started, and before long the cancer seemed to be in remission.

It was during this pause in the illness that the next curiously specific object lesson occurred. One day in May of 1961, eight years after that first mescaline-aided cleansing of the doors of his perception, Huxley was on the second floor of his house, typing away on the last pages of *Island,* his utopian Life Manual about a community in the South Seas where wisdom—complete with hallucinogen-aided initiations for young people—is a genuinely lived reality. Work came to a halt when he learned that a brushfire, of the sort that periodically sweeps through the Hollywood Hills, was raging nearby. It soon became apparent that the fire might move in the direction of the Huxley household.

"Aldous was right," Laura later wrote of this day. "The fire was about to choose our home, beginning to burn the plants on the slope under the terrace. Aldous went upstairs and got his almost finished manuscript of *Island;* he had started it five years before, when we moved into the house, and had been working steadily on it for the last two years. When he came down he said, 'Don't you think I should take some suits?'

"I said, 'Yes.'

"But I was looking—and only looking. How beautiful everything was! The flames from the outside were giving to the white walls a soft rosy glow. That very day I had changed the flowers. In a large vase a triumphant bunch of 'hot pokers' were illuminated from inside and out. The simplicity of the decorations, the shining liquid whiteness of the floors, the few objects—everything was given a glowing life by the dancing flames outside."

Randomly jumping from bush to bush, the fire made its way toward the house where a lifetime's worth of diligent and inspired scholarship lay stored up—and when it had passed, nothing was left behind. Or rather almost nothing. The fire that took virtually the entire material evidence of Huxley's life and achievements from him in a matter of hours left two items entirely untouched: a box of unwanted books he had recently culled from his library to give to charity and a stack of firewood.

Once back on their feet from the fire, the Huxleys made plans for a trip to Europe. Huxley continued with his writing and lectured to large and enthusiastic audiences on mescaline, enlightenment, and the truths of the perennial philosophy. Yet as he did so, and even as the public appetite for the things he was saying seemed to take on a new and unprecedented intensity, Huxley himself was growing weaker. The cancer had returned.

By the end of 1962 it was obvious to everyone—save, perhaps, Huxley himself—that he was terribly ill. Whenever possible, the cancer was not referred to by name at all. Laura, meanwhile, found herself increasingly at a loss for how to deal with Huxley's condition, given the fact that he was so determined to ignore it. Even when Huxley's first wife, Maria, was desperately sick, Laura wrote, "Aldous had not realized that the end was near. When the doctor told him, only a few days before the end, that there was nothing more to be done, the news had come as a shock to him. 'You see, I did not realize Maria was dying . . . '

"And now, does he know that *he* is dying?"

Life, neither simply good nor simply bad, but both in spades: demanding to be lived but also to be seen through with total equanimity, so that the other, larger thing behind it may at last come into view—that hidden landscape that the wisdom traditions of every country and every period of history have known about and ceaselessly reminded people of. It had been Huxley's own great desire to remind the world of the centrality and seriousness of that landscape. It now fell to him to spend his final days in a direct, and agonizingly immediate, encounter with it.

"If I Get Out of This"

Huxley's condition continued to worsen, and by the fall of 1963 he was completely bedridden. Nursing him and helping him with his work, Laura continued to watch for the moment when Huxley was ready to face what to everyone else was obvious: he was dying. Yet week after week, the admission didn't come. It was not, she realized, that Huxley was choosing to battle the illness with positive thinking. He was simply refusing to face a reality that, though overwhelmingly evident, was too much for him to cope with.

"During the last two months," Laura wrote, "I gave him almost daily an opportunity, an opening, for speaking about death, but of course this opening was always one that could have been taken in two ways—either toward life or toward death; and he always took it toward life. We read the entire manual of Dr. Leary based on the Tibetan Book of the Dead. He could have, even jokingly, said: 'Don't forget to remind me when the time comes.' His comment instead was directed only to the problem of 're-entry' after a psychedelic session. It is true he sometimes said things like, 'If I get out of this,' in connection with his new ideas of writing, and wondered when and if he would have the strength to work. He was mentally very active and it seemed that some new levels of his mind were stirring."

A Moment of Truth

The final decade of Huxley's life concluded, as it had begun, with a hallucinogen. After weeks in bed, always hinting and hoping that the disease would relent and allow him to get back on his feet, Huxley arrived at a moment in which he seems at last to have been able to look directly at the truth. It was a moment that had been a long time in coming; but it was also one that, late or not, gives the story of Huxley's final days a strange yet powerful note of triumph.

On the morning of November 22, 1963—the day of John F. Kennedy's assassination, and the last day of Huxley's life as well—Laura found him increasingly uncomfortable. "All of a sudden—it must have been then ten o'clock—he could hardly speak, and he whispered he wanted 'a big, big piece of paper to write on.' I did not want to leave the room to find it, so I took a typewriter tablet that was near by, laid it on a large tray and held it. Aldous wrote, 'If I go,' and gave a direction for his will."

The significance of these three simple words were not lost on Laura.

" 'If I go.' This was the first time he had said that with reference to *now*. He wrote it. I knew and felt that for the first time he was looking at death—now."

Shortly after this Huxley again asked for his pad and with difficulty wrote the words "Try LSD 100 mm intramuscular." Huxley had never abandoned his faith in the efficacy of hallucinogens as tools for the intensification of understanding—and with this request Laura got confirmation that he at last knew and accepted that the end was near. Laura brought the drug and a syringe to Huxley's bedside and, with trembling hands, administered the shot.

"I just sat there without speaking for a while. Aldous was not so agitated physically. He seemed—somehow I felt he knew— we both knew what we were doing, and this had always been a great relief to Aldous. I have seen him at times during his illness upset until he knew what he was going to do, then, the decision taken, however serious, he would make a total change. This enormous feeling of relief would come to him, and he wouldn't be worried about it at all. He would say let's do it, and we would do it, and he was like a liberated man. And now I had the same feeling: a decision had been made. Suddenly he had accepted the fact of death."

No Magic Tricks

Almost up until that final day, Huxley had been struggling, with Laura's help, to complete an essay commissioned by *Show* magazine called "Shakespeare and Religion." Huxley did in fact manage to complete it, dictating the last paragraphs into a tape recorder when he became too weak to write. Within this last completed work, composed with such great effort, one passage stands out. In light of the condition Huxley was in when he created it, it is not altogether out of line to read it as a final statement, made with utmost earnestness and coming from the very depths of his experience, of what, to his mind, wisdom truly is.

"The world is an illusion," said Huxley into that tape recorder, just days before his death. "But it is an illusion which we must take seriously, because it is real as far as it goes, and in those aspects of the reality which we are capable of apprehending. Our business is to wake up. We have to find ways in which to detect the whole of reality in the one illusory part which our self-centered consciousness permits us to see. We must not live thoughtlessly, taking our illusion for the complete reality, but at the same time we must not live too thoughtfully in the sense of trying to escape from the dream state. We must continually be on our watch for ways in which we may enlarge our consciousness. We must not attempt to live outside the world, which is given us, but we must somehow learn how to transform it and transfigure it. Too much 'wisdom' is as bad as too little wisdom, and there must be no magic tricks. We must learn to come to reality without the enchanter's wand and his book of the words. One must find a way of being in this world while not being in it. A way of living in time without being completely swallowed up in time."

Huxley spent the better half of his life journeying toward these words, and the living truth behind them. And in the final moments of that life, it would seem, he stepped into that truth completely.

Further Discoveries About Relationship

Our need for other people is paradoxical.

—THE DALAI LAMA

In the fall of 1981, following the summer of my cross-country trip, I got a job in New York City, as a messenger boy in Elena's father's investment counseling company. Having sampled the road less traveled and come up short, it occurred to me that I might learn something from taking a reverse tack and placing myself right within the very heart of conventionality. It was, as I saw it, a sort of judo maneuver—an attempt to learn, by submitting to them, the secrets of the very forces I had set myself against.

Riding the subway up and down between Wall Street and midtown with a wad of stock tickets in one hand and a Life Manual in the other, I marveled at how much easier, on some levels at least, this new honest, wage-earning existence of mine was than all the months of labor-intensive loafing that had preceded it. To my great interest, I learned that office life really was by and large what I had for so long heard it to be: an endless round of essentially pointless tasks, punctuated by people talking about things like who made the coffee, whether everybody had seen the game the night before, and similarly inane stuff, day after day, week in and week out. For once, my literature had given me a truly accurate picture of what greeted me in reality. It was all just as curiously flat and inconclusive as Henry Miller and Jack Kerouac and Robert Pirsig and the rest of them had promised me it was.

One day, a month or so into this new, weirdly normal lifestyle, Elena called from college and told me she didn't want to be my girlfriend anymore. It just wasn't working, she said. I was too self-involved, too wrapped up with all of my assorted preoccupations. We didn't have, she explained to me, a real *relationship*. And without a real relationship there really wasn't much point in continuing the way we had.

It was the sort of phone call one could imagine don Juan or don Genaro getting from his girlfriend. To be a man of knowledge, you had to cut yourself off from the world; you had to be alone. For such a man, relationship—at least of the interpersonal sort—was in fact the *problem*, not the solution, and you couldn't expect someone who wasn't out to become an Adult Unlike Other Adults themselves to understand this. It only took a moment of thinking about it for me to realize Elena had done the right thing. Who could blame her for losing patience?

But the thing was, once I hung up and got back about my business, I started to get this funny kind of feeling—a feeling that I really liked Elena quite a lot more, and in a different sort of way, than I'd ever noticed I did until right now. I'd pretty much made my peace with being attached to her and all that, but all of a sudden something different from attachment—something not quite so easy to pinpoint and define—seemed to have snuck into the picture. Along with this realization came a remarkably deep and untheoretical feeling of depression—one that settled down upon me like a sudden snow out of a formerly clear blue sky.

After a day or so of feeling depressed like this, I called Elena to give her the good news that maybe we shouldn't be so quick about ending our relationship, such as it was, after all. Perhaps she too wanted to change her mind? Unfortunately, however, Elena didn't want to. Not that day, nor the next when I called again. Nor the day after that either.

To my dismay, I now found that where beforehand my job—with its endless filing and its subway trips and all the rest—had been dispiriting in a novel and anthropological sort of way, it was now crushingly, relentlessly, suffocatingly so. Previously I had been a mere tourist in the land of wage-earning normalcy. Now, with Elena's departure, it seemed I was being handed my permanent papers of residence. The daily tedium that I had initially studied from a distance took on an altogether new, and altogether unpleasant, density and intimacy. A part of my life was gone—one that I had never quite managed to understand was important to me when it was actually there—and with it had departed a certain happiness, perhaps even a kind of innocence, that I had also not realized was there while I had it.

I dimly remembered reading something about this phenomenon in my Life Manuals. The idea was that people by nature only realized what made them happy once they didn't have it anymore. But knowing that the experience had been documented and cataloged did not do anything to make it less unpleasant. In fact, this knowledge might just have made it a little more so.

One night, after a week or two of getting more and more depressed, I called Nicky to tell him about what had happened with Elena and to ask for his advice. He was completely understanding. For in fact, he said, the feelings I was having now were really the same ones that had first led him to become a Buddhist. This pain I felt—this sense of absence and betrayal and confusion—were what he had come to believe life was all about at its heart, and it was quite likely that I was experiencing this feeling now, in its undiluted form, for the first time ever. Living meant getting attached to things, only to have those things taken away. It meant feeling the terrible pain of that absence, until something else came along and took the place of the thing that was gone. Then the whole business started over, again and again, without end. It was only when a person stopped and looked and understood with open eyes that life was really like this that they could start to change: to become something genuinely other than what they had been. The pain itself was the first key to the first door that led, eventually, to freedom.

After a couple of months the initial effects of Elena's cancellation of our nonrelationship wore off, and I no longer walked about doing my messenger duties with that intense, heavy sadness pressing down upon me. But it still pretty much stunk, being a messenger boy, and if this was what normal people did all their lives, I realized I could still use a little more preparation time for dealing with this fact. So one day I called my father up and asked how the finances were going and if he could maybe pay for another year or two of college somewhere before he went totally bust. And my father said yes, that could probably be worked out. So I decided I would go back to school, and this time around I wouldn't worry so much about Cartesian dualism and the Western tradition and all that stuff I'd been so wrapped up with the last time. I would just take some courses and see what happened—and be grateful that I wasn't on that damn subway heading down to Wall Street anymore, or listening to someone talk about who made the coffee, or any of the rest of it. And if the Judeo-Christian, Newtonian-Cartesian tradition ended up taking me over and brainwashing me, so it would just have to be. But it probably wouldn't anyhow.

An Incident on the Beach

Wherever his way may take him, the pupil, though he may lose sight of his teacher, can never forget him. With a gratitude as great as the uncritical veneration of the beginner, as strong as the saving faith of the artist, he now takes his Master's place, ready for any sacrifice. Countless examples down to the recent past testify that this gratitude far exceeds the measure of what is customary among mankind.

—EUGEN HERRIGEL

It is no good asking for a simple religion.

—C. S. LEWIS

One day on the beach out on Long Island in the early weeks of 1982, a short while after I had gone back to school, I was walking along with Nicky and his teacher, Rinpoche—a reincarnated Tibetan lama who had emigrated to the States back in the sixties, and who had recently become both Nicky's primary Buddhist teacher and his friend. It was a windy, over-cast day, and the clouds overhead seemed to amplify the sound made by the large, rough waves coming in from the sea. Suddenly Nicky, who was walking a little ahead of me and talking to Rinpoche, pointed out at the water. Just beyond where the waves were breaking, a dark, round, massive object was lolling about.

As we stood and watched, the waves slowly pushed the thing—which we now could see was an animal of some sort—closer into shore. In a minute it was past the line where the surf broke, so that each wave that came in tumbled it end over end. Occasionally it seemed to try to right itself, but the movements did no good, and the waves kept on slapping and shoving it ever farther in toward the sand.

"You know about fish," Nicky said to me. "What kind do you suppose that is?"

"I think it's a mola—a sunfish. They live in the open ocean. I've only seen them in books. Their body is kind of like a big head, with a fin at the top and the bottom. I don't think that they belong that close in. This one must be sick or something."

I gave Nicky my wallet, and without bothering to remove my shoes or roll up my pants, waded out toward the animal. Taking long steps through the freezing waves, I got closer and closer. Yes, it was a mola all right. Through the dark water I could see its mouth opening and closing, and a large, staring, melancholy eye. What could I do for it? Nothing. All the same, I kept moving. Then, just as I was about to reach out and place my hand on it, something happened. In a flash, the fish righted itself and sank down swiftly beneath the waves. Where a moment before it had seemed hopelessly weak and out of place, it was now all strength and coherence, swimming power-fully away from me. In a moment it was gone.

Back on the beach, standing numb in my wet clothes next to Nicky and Rinpoche, I looked out at the water.

"What happened?" said Nicky.

"I don't know. . . . That was weird. There was *definitely* something wrong with that fish. But when I got out to it, it just took off like it was fine."

"You made the fish get better," said Rinpoche in his odd, whispery, almost incomprehensible English.

"That was really odd," I said again to Nicky as we continued on our walk, Rinpoche moving ahead of us now, his mustard and maroon robes flapping in the wind.

"It's an odd world," Nicky said.

"No, I mean it. It's like that fish just woke up and came to its senses all of a sudden. It swam away like a rocket."

Nicky motioned to Rinpoche as he walked along ahead of us. "You heard what he said."

Despite his intriguing status as a multiply reincarnated, genuinely enlightened being, I had so far found it somewhat difficult to talk to Rinpoche on the couple of occasions when I had seen him with Nicky. My hard-learned rule of being suspicious of any presumably wise being who was actually present in three dimensions, rather than on the page of one of my beloved Life Manuals, continued to stand. In addition, Rinpoche's English made him exceptionally difficult to communicate with—at least for me, for unlike Nicky I could barely understand what he was talking about most of the time. But I knew that Nicky set great store by him, and I certainly understood what he was getting at now.

"You really think something fixed that fish, don't you?"

We kept on walking, and I thought about it. Who was to say? Maybe Rinpoche had fixed the fish. Maybe I had even played a part in the event myself somehow, as Rinpoche had suggested. It was an interesting idea. And equally interesting, to me, was the notion that Nicky was so entirely ready to believe Rinpoche's words on such a matter. He really had faith in this odd, incomprehensible little guy. For all that I had read about such relationships, it was surprising—and perhaps still a bit unbelievable—to see one actually going on right before my eyes.

Nicky was now preparing himself for the vows of monkhood. A few short years later, he would be living at a monastery in India as a full-fledged, full-time, no-holds-barred Buddhist. I, in turn, had come to decide, even more than I had before, that this Buddhism of his really wasn't for me. I just couldn't get my head around all that emptiness stuff, for all that I might try. But that didn't mean I respected what Nicky was doing any the less. I knew he was doing what all the really serious people in the world had always done, wisdom-wise. You had to find the road that really suited you—the "path with heart" that the fictional don Juan had told Carlos and me about at the very beginning of my wisdom adventures—and once you did so you had to start walking, and keep quiet, and follow directions, and just sort of hope for the best.

The really tricky thing—maybe the trickiest of all—was that you had to turn yourself completely over to the process before you even knew where it was going. That was the one thing, I now understood, that you just *had* to do. Because if you didn't—if you tried to call the shots ahead of time and make the road go the way you *thought* it should go instead of the way it actually did—it would just vanish before your eyes. Like the Egyptian goddess Neith behind her veil that no one has ever lifted, or like Emperor Hun Tun dying in the arms of Emperors Hu and Shu, or even like that strange, giant fish that had just swum away from us, it would all just disappear back to the place from which it had come. A place you could never really see from the normal world no matter how hard you tried, but that was always right out there all the same—alive, and awake, and watching, for all its invisibility.

NOTES

INTRODUCTION

   p. 3: E. F. Schumacher, *A Guide for the Perplexed*, Harper & Row, 1977, p. 139.

CHAPTER ONE

   p. 16: All quotations from the *Tao-te Ching*, translated by James Legge, from *The Texts of Taoism*, Oxford University Press, 1891. Reprinted by Dover Books, 1962. p. 18: Herlee G. Creel, "On Two Aspects in Early Taoism." Reprinted in *What Is Taoism? And Other Studies in Chinese Cultural History*, University of Chicago Press, 1970, p. 42. p. 19: Toshihiko Izutsu, *Sufism and Taoism: A Comparative Study of Key Philosophical Ideas*, University of California Press, 1984, p. 304. p. 22: "If we live . . ." from Alan Watts, "Beat Zen, Square Zen, and Zen."© 1958 Alan Watts, p. 5. "The ego is neither . . ." from Alan Watts, *In My Own Way: An Autobiography*, Pantheon Books, 1972, p. 251. p. 22: "[A] continuous, self-moving stream . . ." from Alan Watts, *Nature, Man and Woman*, Pantheon Books, 1958, p. 70. p. 25: Aldous Huxley, *The Doors of Perception*, HarperCollins, 1954, 1990, p. 17. p. 26: Ibid.

CHAPTER TWO

   p. 37: All quotations from The Bhagavad Gita from *The Song of God: The Bhagavad* see p. vii, *Gita*, translated by Swami Prabhavananda and Christopher Isherwood, The Vedanta Press, 1944, 1951, pp. 63, 51, 44, 39, 44, 68, 39. p. 42: Robert Pirsig, *Zen and the Art of Motorcycle Maintenance: An Enquiry into Values*, William Morrow & Co., 1974, p. 42.

NOTES

p. 46: Huxley, *Doors*, p. 62. p. 55: Richard Wilhelm and Caryl F. Baynes, *The I Ching, or Book of Changes*, Bollingen/Princeton University Press, 1922, p. 52.

CHAPTER THREE

p. 61: The Apocryphal Book of Ben Sirach (Ecclesiasticus) 24:29, quoted in Anne Baring and Jules Cashford, *The Myth of the Goddess*, Penguin/Arkana, 1991, p. 187. p. 62 "No mortal hath lifted my veil," quoted in Huntington Cairns, *The Limits of Art*, Bollingen, 1947, p. 49. All quotations from *The Consolation of Philosophy* by Boethius, translated, with introduction and notes, by Richard Green, Library of Liberal Arts, 1962, 1980, Pp. 21, 31, 41.

CHAPTER FOUR

p. 71: All quotations from Eugen Herrigel from *Zen in the Art of Archery*, Pantheon Books, 1999, pp. 32, 38, 69. p. 80: J. Krishnamurti, *The Awakening of Intelligence*, HarperCollins, 1973, p. 315. p. 98: Richard Carlson, Ph.D., *Don't Sweat the Small Stuff . . . And It's All Small Stuff*, Hyperion, 1997, p. 39.

CHAPTER FIVE

p. 107: Aldous Huxley, *The Perennial Philosophy*, Harper & Brothers, 1945, p. 117. p. 108 Henry Miller, *Tropic of Capricorn*, Grove Press, 1939, p. 1. p. 112: Ibid. p. 115: Julia Cameron, *The Artist's Way*, Jeremy P. Tarcher, 1992, p. 55. p. 117: Natalie Goldberg, *Writing Down the Bones*, Shambhala Publications, 1986, p. 9. p. 121: Plato, *Philebus*, p. 530. p. 122: Robert Fulghum, *All I Really Needed to Know I Learned in Kindergarten*, Villard Books, 1993, p. 129. p. 125: Dr. Wayne W. Dyer, *Everyday Wisdom*, Hay House, 1993, p. 28.

CHAPTER SIX

p. 129: All quotations from Black Elk from *Black Elk Speaks: Being the Life Story of a Holy Man of the Oglala Sioux*, by John G. Neihardt, University of Nebraska Press, 1988, Pp. 18, 36. p. 132: James Redfield, *The Celestine Prophecy: An Adventure*, Warner Books, 1994, p. 37. p. 141:

NOTES

François Fénelon quoted in Aldous Huxley, *The Perennial Philosophy*, Harper & Brothers, 1945, p. 114. p. 154: H. Jackson Brown, Jr., *Life's Little Instruction Book*, Rutledge Hill Press, 1991, p. 174. p. 160: Steven Foster and Meredith Little, "The Vision Quest: Passing from Childhood to Adulthood," from *Betwixt & Between: Patterns of Masculine and Feminine Initiation*, edited by Louise Carus Mahdi, Steven Foster, and Meredith Little, Open Court, 1981, p. 85. p. 163: Ibid.

CHAPTER SEVEN

p. 177: Carlos Castaneda, *Journey to Ixtlan*, Simon & Schuster, 1972, p. 264. p. 181: Kahlil Gibran, *Visions of the Prophet*, Frog, Ltd., 1997. p. 195: Louise Carus Mahdi, from the introduction to *Betwixt & Between*, p. xiii. William Law quoted in Aldous Huxley, *The Perennial Philosophy*, Harper & Brothers, 1945, p. 243. p. 202: From an interview with Juliette Huxley, quoted in *Huxley in Hollywood* by David King Dunaway, Harper & Row, 1989, p. 309. Heracleitus (Herakleitos) fragment translated by Guy Davenport, *7 Greeks*, New Directions, 1995. p. 203: All quotations from Laura Huxley from *This Timeless Moment* by Laura Huxley, Farrar, Straus and Giroux, 1968, Pp. 69–74, 261, 298–308. p. 207: Aldous Huxley, "Shakespeare and Religion," originally printed in *Show* magazine, Hartford Publishers, Inc., 1964; reprinted in *Huxley and God*, HarperCollins, 1991, p. 279. p. 208: The Dalai Lama and Howard C. Cutler, *The Art of Happiness*, Riverhead Books, 1998, p. 90. p. 212: C. S. Lewis, *Mere Christianity*, Macmillan, 1960, p. 67. Eugen Herrigel from *Zen in the Art of Archery*, Pantheon Books, 1999, pp. 32, 38, 69.

INDEX

INDEX

Buddhism, Buddhists, 30, 40, 58,
65, 75, 81, 88, 108, 123,
180, 186, 211
see also Tibetan Buddhism; Zen
Buddhism
Bynner, Witter, 13, 15

Cameron, Julia, 115
Capra, Fritjof, 37
Carlson, Richard, 98
Cartagena, 74, 81–85
Castaneda, Carlos, 6, 29, 99,
131, 142, 143, 145, 149,
167, 177, 179, 180, 196,
199, 200, 215
Catcher in the Rye, The (Salinger),
8
Catholicism, 198
Celestine Prophecy, The (Redfield),
132
chaos, see Hun Tun
chaos theory, 18
chévere, 84, 110, 117
Cheyenne rites of passage, 160,
163
Christianity, 9–10, 48, 65
Chuang-tzu, 23, 24, 40
Chuang-tzu, 18, 19
Cigarettes, Tao of, 153–54
Colombia, 74, 78, 81–85, 88,
95, 97, 98–106, 107–8,
117, 131, 149
Confucius, 54
Consolation of Philosophy, The
(Boethius), 63–65
Copernicus, Nicolaus, 34, 35

creativity, enlightenment
through, 120–21, 123–24
Creel, Herlee G., 18

Dalai Lama, 77, 208
Darwin, Charles, 35
Descartes, René, 35, 65
don Juan, see Matus, don Juan
Don't Sweat the Small Stuff . . . And
It's All Small Stuff (Carlson),
98
Doors of Perception, The (Huxley),
25–27, 46, 145, 169, 200
dualism, 31, 35
Dunaway, David King, 202
Dyer, Wayne W., 125

Ecclesiastes, Book of, 1
ego, 22, 26, 29, 36, 111, 114,
121, 123
Egypt, ancient, 62
Elena (author's girlfriend),
58–59, 66, 108, 118,
139–40, 164, 208–11
Emerson, Ralph Waldo, 44, 95,
198
enlightenment, 88, 95–96, 107,
121, 188
Everyday Wisdom (Dyer), 125

Fénelon, François, 141
floaters, 185, 192–93
flux, universe as characterized
by, 18
Foster, Steven, 160, 163
Franny and Zooey (Salinger), 8

INDEX

299.93
T

Tompkins, Ptolemy.

The beaten path.

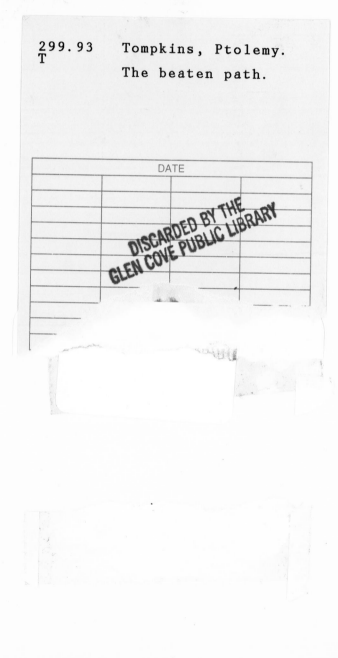